In Nature's Interests?

Environmental Ethics and Science Policy Series
GENERAL EDITOR: KRISTIN SCHRADER-FRECHETTE

In Nature's Interests?

Interests, Animal Rights, and Environmental Ethics

GARY E. VARNER

New York   Oxford
Oxford University Press
1998

Oxford University Press

Oxford   New York
Athens   Auckland   Bangkok   Bogotá   Buenos Aires   Calcutta
Cape Town   Chennai   Dar es Salaam   Delhi   Florence   Hong Kong   Istanbul
Karachi   Kuala Lumpur   Madrid   Melbourne   Mexico City   Mumbai
Nairobi   Paris   São Paulo   Singapore   Taipei   Tokyo   Toronto   Warsaw

and associated companies in
Berlin   Ibadan

Copyright © 1998 by Gary E. Varner

Published by Oxford University Press, Inc.
198 Madison Avenue, New York, New York 10016

Oxford is a registered trademark of Oxford University Press.

Library of Congress Cataloging-in-Publication Data
Varner, Gary E. (Gary Edward), 1957–
    In nature's interests? : interests, animal rights, and
environmental ethics / Gary E. Varner.
        p.   cm.—(Environmental ethics and science policy series)
    Includes bibliographical references and index.
    ISBN 0-19-510865-5
    1. Environmental ethics.   2. Animal rights.   3. Environmentalists—
Attitude.   4. Philosophy of nature.   I.   Title.   Series:
Environmental ethics and science policy.
GE42.V38   1998
179'.1—dc21   97-28389

9 8 7 6 5 4 3 2 1
Printed in the United States of America
on acid-free paper

FOR NANCI AND SPUNKY

who take no interest in such things

Acknowledgments

A NUMBER of readers and audiences provided me with valuable feedback during the composition of this book.

Chapters 2, 3, and 4 began as chapters in my doctoral dissertation, which was finally completed a year after my advisor, Jon Moline, had left the University of Wisconsin-Madison to become Vice President and Dean of St. Olaf College in Northfield, Minnesota. I appreciated the way Jon stuck with that project while both his mind and his body were elsewhere.

Most of the chapters have benefited from being presented in whole or in part to philosophy departments or conferences. Parts of chapter 1 were presented to the Mountains-Plains Philosophical Association's annual meeting (October 1991) and to the International Society for Environmental Ethics (December 1991) under the titles "No Sympathy for Systems: Humean–Smithian Moral Psychology and the Foundations of the Leopold Land Ethic" and "A Critique of Environmental Holism," respectively. Versions of chapter 2 were presented to the Illinois Philosophical Association's annual meeting (October 1987) and to the philosophy departments at Washington University in St. Louis (1988) and Texas A&M University (1990). A version of chapter 3 was presented to the Philosophy Department at Texas A&M University (spring 1989) as part of a job interview. A version of chapter 4 was presented (spring 1993) to the same department after they gave me a job. I'm glad they gave me a job. It's been a nice place to teach and write.

Over the years, I have also benefited from informal discussions of the positions defended in this book, especially with my very constructively critical colleague Colin Allen, and with Edwin Hettinger, Bill Throop, and Gary Comstock, who seem to turn up at the same conferences I do. And late in the process of composition, Richard "Red" Watson sloughed through the entire manuscript, spilled barrels of red ink on it, and forced me to eliminate forms of speech with unintended ontological implications.

Portions of the manuscript have appeared previously in print. Much of chapter 3 and almost all of chapter 5 appeared as (respectively) "Biological Functions and Biological Interests," *Southern Journal of Philosophy* 27 (1990): 251–70, and

"Can Animal Rights Activists Be Environmentalists?" in Donald Marietta and Lester Embree, eds., *Environmental Philosophy and Environmental Activism* (Lanham, Md.: Rowman & Littlefield, 1995), 169–201. Both are reprinted in Donald VanDeVeer and Christine Pierce, eds., *People, Penguins, and Plastic Trees*, 2nd ed. (Belmont, Calif.: Wadsworth, 1994). Small portions of chapters 1 and 5 appeared in my review of Eugene C. Hargrove, *The Animal Rights/Environmental Ethics Debate: The Environmental Perspective* (Albany: State University of New York Press, 1992), in *Environmental Ethics* 15 (1993): 279–82. Some of the material from chapter 6 was temporarily available as a discussion paper from Texas A&M's Center for Biotechnology Policy and Ethics, under the title "Environmental Ethics: Conservation or Preservation?" I am indebted to the Center's Director, Paul Thompson, for funding a half-time release from teaching during the 1990–91 and 1991–92 academic years, during which the introduction and chapter 1 were written.

Contents

In Nature's Interests?

Interests, Holism, and Environmental Ethics

As I CONCEIVE OF IT, ethical behavior produces and preserves value in the world. A morally good person knows what has value and acts to produce and preserve it. This book articulates and defends a particular vision of what has value and therefore of the morally good life: the view that the satisfaction of interests is of primary and overriding moral value.

In the 1990s, it has become common to make appeals to what is in *nature's* interests. In 1990, the editors of *Audubon* magazine began describing it on its masthead as "Speaking for Nature." On the twentieth anniversary of the original Earth Day, David Brower's autobiography was published with the title *For Earth's Sake*. A book called *Fifty Simple Things You Can Do to Save the Earth* went to the top of the nonfiction bestseller list. And in the wake of Earth Day 1990, a surprising range of companies began describing themselves or their products as "Environment Friendly" (President's Choice), "Kind to the Earth" (K-Mart), or "Taking Bold Steps for Earth" (Turner Broadcasting System). The language of both environmentalists and businesses in the 1990s suggests that both human beings and nature have interests in some literal sense, interests that can come to loggerheads.

Appeals to what is in nature's interests certainly have achieved a kind of rhetorical hegemony, but sometimes the rhetoric is metaphorical. A popular poster displays a photograph of the earth taken from one of the Apollo moon shots and urges you to "Love Your Mother." One is unsure how literally to take this admonition. The paradigm case of love, that between adult human beings, involves recognition of and concern for the interests of the object of one's love. One does not really love one's spouse unless one is committed to advancing his or her interests. But one can "love" something, in a looser and more metaphorical sense, without thinking that the object of one's "love" has interests. I use this looser sense of the term when I say that I love a good strong cup of coffee first thing in the morning or that I love an old photograph of my friends. I can love coffee and a photograph in this weaker, more metaphorical sense, without thinking that either coffee or a photograph has interests that I could further or set back. The only interests at stake are mine, not the coffee's or the photograph's.

The label on a "green" product distributed by the Fort Howard Paper Company contains a use of "love" in such a purely metaphorical way:

> If you love nature, you'll appreciate Green Forest Bathroom Tissue. Made from 100% recycled fibers, Green Forest is made to the highest standards without compromising precious natural resources. This soft tissue is perfect for tender skin. And with our 360-sheet two-ply roll, you get 20% more sheets than with most premium brands. So Green Forest is the right choice for your family because it's as good for them as it is for nature.

The overriding message is clear: this toilet paper is good for both you and nature. It is good for you, because it satisfies various relevant interests, such as economy and comfort. It is also in some sense "good for nature," but it sounds as if this is to be taken in the same sense as something being good for a photograph one "loves." The label refers to "precious natural resources." A resource is something you use, and because it has a use, you value it. But nothing on the Fort Howard label suggests that nature—anymore than a treasured photograph—literally has interests. So sometimes talking about "Environment Friendly" products and urging people to "Be Kind to the Earth" is like saying "easy does it" to someone handling a delicate vase. The interests at stake are, strictly speaking, ours, not the vase's—or nature's.

Other times, however, the rhetoric of nature's interests is not meant metaphorically. In March 1990, an environmental group called Friends of the River took out full-page ads in major newspapers to urge the Department of the Interior to stop altering radically the release rate from Glen Canyon Dam in response to daily fluctuations in electrical demand. "The Grand Canyon is fighting for its life," they said in the ad. "The natural beauty and long-term health of Grand Canyon National Park is more important than squeezing the last kilowatt from Glen Canyon Dam." Although it is difficult to be certain how to interpret such statements, to talk of the "life" and "health" of the Grand Canyon is to suggest that it literally has interests more strongly than does the Fort Howard Paper label's reference to "precious natural resources." Surely one cannot be friends with a river in the same way that one can be friends with a fellow human being or even a companion animal, but the contrast drawn in the ad between thinking of the river as merely a resource ("squeezing the last kilowatt" from it) and thinking of its own health suggests much more strongly than the Fort Howard advertisement that the Friends of the River think the river itself has interests.

Appeals to what is in nature's interests are attractive to those in the environmental movement, because so many environmental activists and environmental philosophers have come to accept as a truism the claim that only by achieving a sort of philosophical paradigm shift can an "environmental crisis" be averted or (if the crisis is conceived of as being already upon us) significantly ameliorated. Denis Hayes, national coordinator of the first Earth Day, held in April 1970, reflected this belief when he described the goal of the event in these terms: "We hoped it would lead to a new kind of ideology, a new value system based on ecology and a reverence for life" (*New York Times*, 16 April 1990). The authors of the first *World Conservation Strategy*, published in 1980, similarly claimed that

> Ultimately the behavior of entire societies towards the biosphere must be trans-
> formed if the achievement of conservation objectives is to be assured. A new
> ethic, embracing plants and animals as well as people, is required for human
> societies to live in harmony with the natural world on which they depend for
> survival and wellbeing. The long term task of environmental education is to
> foster or reinforce attitudes and behavior compatible with this new ethic. (IUCN,
> 1980)

The claim being made here is that the environmental crisis forces us to reexamine our concept of moral standing. Traditionally, it is claimed, only human beings were thought to matter, morally speaking; but the environmental crisis will not be resolved until we break with tradition and acknowledge that nonhuman nature also has moral standing.

Such appeals to an environmental crisis are conceptually muddled, however. If the crisis is defined anthropocentrically, in terms of a threat to human survival or well-being, then enlightened anthropocentrism requires us to resolve the environmental crisis. No "new" ethic is needed. If, on the other hand, the crisis is defined nonanthropocentrically, in terms of a kind of human mistreatment of nonhuman animals, plants, and ecosystems, then in even saying that there is a crisis we are already assuming an answer to the question of whether nonhuman nature has moral standing, the very question the environmental crisis was invoked to motivate.

A clearer way to proceed is by talking in terms of the extent to which an ethic provides philosophical support for goals commonly espoused in the environmental movement, goals such as:

1. preservation of species, wilderness, and special habitats such as wetlands, estuaries, rain forests, and deserts;
2. reintroduction of locally extinct species including large predators, removal of exotic species, and adaptation of agricultural and landscaping practices to the local biota;
3. substantial reduction of the global human population, and
4. reduced reliance on chemicals in agriculture and reduced air and water emissions.

The claim that many environmentalists make then comes to this: only a non-anthropocentric ethic can provide a strong ethical rationale for pursuing the goals listed on this environmentalist agenda.

In the early 1970s, a series of academic papers by authors making analogous claims were published, papers that shaped the newly emerging field of environmental ethics (Stone 1972; Naess 1973; Routley 1973; and Rolston 1974–75). Environmental philosophers, like environmental activists, have tended to assume that resolution of the environmental crisis will involve a paradigm shift in ethics, and much (if not most) of the work in environmental ethics has been devoted to the question of which nonhuman entities have moral standing.

However, environmental philosophers have shied away from appeals to nature's interests. Although it would be dangerous to say that there is much theoretical consensus among environmental ethicists at this time, one argument has been widely influential:

1. Environmentalists reach the conclusions they do because they are concerned with values that reside in wholes (species, biotic communities, and ecosystems).
2. But only individuals (perhaps only conscious individuals) have interests.
3. Therefore, appeals to what is in nature's interests will not provide firm philosophical support for the environmentalist agenda.

So while environmental activists have continued to use appeals to what is in nature's interests, environmental philosophers have shied away from them.

Appealing to what is in nature's interests will remain a useful rhetorical device, however, because a common way—indeed a central way—of formulating questions about ethics is in terms of impacts on the interests of various affected parties, and at least some interests are commonly thought to have overriding moral weight. Kenneth Goodpaster put the point this way:

> Though [the concept of morality] is not *exhausted* by its inclusion of reference to the *good* and *harm* done to others by an agent, this reference is surely a central part of it. Beneficence and nonmaleficence, then, are not only necessary ingredients in our shared conception of moral (vs. nonmoral) obligation, they are *central*. But one cannot do good for or avoid harm to entities that have no interests. (1980, p. 282)

It is because the concept of others' interests is so closely allied with the concepts of doing harm to and benefiting others that interests are crucial to our thinking about ethics. To say that a being has interests is to say that it has a welfare, or a good of its own, that matters from the moral point of view. This is why the satisfaction of interests constitutes a fundamental moral value. So appealing to the "life" and "health" of the Grand Canyon is a dramatic way of focusing moral scrutiny on Department of the Interior water release practices. The "long-term health of Grand Canyon" would seem to be one of those interests that is indeed "more important than squeezing the last kilowatt from Glen Canyon Dam."

But is it true that appeals to the interests of individuals cannot ground the environmentalist agenda? I do not claim that the satisfaction of interests is the only kind of moral value, but I do think it carries special weight, and, for the reasons given in chapter 1, I believe that the strongest reasons for pursuing the environmentalist agenda will be based, ultimately, on the satisfaction of interests. Chapter 1 is, in a sense, autobiographical. In my first two published papers (1985, 1987), I, like many environmental activists and environmental philosophers, assumed that an ethical argument for pursuing the goals on the environmentalist agenda would have to come from some version of holism.[1] But as I tried to see how such a view could be operationalized, and as I looked more closely at the leading environmental philosophers' own attempts, I discovered deep-seated and, I suspected, ultimately insuperable obstacles. Chapter 1 contains a discussion of these obstacles. Although my argument in the chapter does not provide a decisive refutation of environmental holism (since it does not—and could not—provide a criticism of every possible version of holism), the conclusion I draw from the important philosophical obstacles facing such views is that the environmentalist agenda would be in jeopardy if we had to ground it on holism. It was for this reason that I concluded, several years ago, that biocentric individualism deserves a closer look. This book is my closer look.

I call the view elaborated in this book, according to which all and only individual living organisms have morally considerable interests, "biocentric individualism."[2] While biocentric in the sense of being both decidedly nonanthropocentric and more inclusive than an animal rights perspective, my view is still squarely within the interest-based, individualist tradition that so many environmental philosophers have claimed cannot generate a strongly environmentalist

1. In a more recent paper, which forms the basis for chapter 3 of this book, I continued to express a related worry. I wrote: "I am increasingly convinced that the intuitions of the environmental movement are best unpacked in terms of an ethical commitment to the preservation of aesthetic value. . . . As an individual who is intuitively and politically committed to the more idealistic goals of the environmental movement, however, I worry that these goals cannot be harmonized with the equally intuitive principle that the protection of interests takes precedence over the preservation of beauty" (Varner 1990, p. 270, n. 42). While the intuitions of environmentalists might well prove to be aesthetic (that is an empirical question), I am now convinced that pursuit of the goals on the environmentalist agenda is best defended in terms of the protection and promotion of the most important interests of human individuals, precisely because aesthetic considerations are relatively weak in relation to the protection of those interests.

2. It is slightly inaccurate to label my view "biocentric," because in chapter 2 I do recognize the possibility of sufficiently complex artifacts having interests, if they meet the functional criteria for having desires that I defend in that chapter. However, I presume that no artificial intelligence produced to date meets those criteria.

ethic. On my view, there are many beings in nature whose interests can be affected by environmental policy, but it makes no sense to speak of what is in nature's interests where the reference of "nature" is a species, biotic community, ecosystem, or other holistic entity. On my view, only individual living organisms have interests. My goal in this book is to articulate clearly the biocentric individualist stance and to defend it against the most common theoretical objections raised against it, including the claim that it cannot ground good environmental policy.

In chapters 2 and 3, I discuss the nature and scope of interests in human beings and in nature. I argue that, although the paradigm cases of interests are defined by reference to the desires of conscious, "higher" organisms (primarily mammals and birds), an exhaustive account of these beings' welfare involves reference to "biological interests," which can be meaningfully predicated of nonconscious organisms (such as plants and "lower" animals such as invertebrates) but not species, biotic communities, or ecosystems.

In chapter 4, I defend the use of Ralph Barton Perry's "principle of inclusiveness" to evaluate individual welfare and to adjudicate conflicts among interests. Although my view is strongly nonanthropocentric insofar as I recognize the moral standing of all living organisms, I argue that Perry's principle of inclusiveness supports what I call "axiological anthropocentrism": the view that a certain class of human interests are more important than the interests of any (or at least almost every) nonhuman organism. I label my view "axiological" anthropocentrism to distinguish it from views that deny nonhuman organisms all direct moral standing. Such views I label "valuationally" anthropocentric.

In chapters 5 and 6, I discuss the environmental implications both of individualist and axiologically anthropocentric stances like mine. In chapter 5, I focus on the claim that, because they are individualistic, animal rights philosophies are inconsistent with the goals of environmentalists. If environmental philosophers have approached consensus on any point, it is that animal rights philosophies are inconsistent with sound environmental policy and in particular with environmentally sound control of wildlife populations. Focusing on the views of Peter Singer and Tom Regan, I argue that animal activists can consistently support hunting in every situation in which environmentalists feel compelled to support it. Although my own views are in the background in this chapter, it concludes with a brief discussion of the principle of inclusiveness and predation and the place of predation in human nature specifically.

In chapter 6, I return to the environmentalist agenda to argue that, in light of an empirical claim that is both central to Aldo Leopold's mature land management philosophy and broadly endorsed by environmentalists, the axiological anthropocentrism defended in chapter 4 supports every plank of the environmentalist agenda. The broadly endorsed claim is: safeguarding humans' continued prosecution of their most important interests requires preservation everywhere of remnants of the original, naturally evolved biota and, in more-fragile ecosystems, approximation of land use practices to the original biota. I describe the way Aldo Leopold arrived at this conclusion and then show why it supports each plank in the environmentalist agenda.

If the argument of this book is sound, the anthropocentrism–nonanthropocentrism dichotomy makes little difference in environmental matters (at least where a sufficiently broad range of human interests is taken into account, and across a sufficiently broad time frame), but it may make an important difference where domesticated or captive animals are concerned. In short, not only are environmentalism and "animal rights" compatible, but also they can—contrary to the conventional wisdom in both areas—be grounded in the same interests-based moral individualism.

That is the central practical thesis of this book, but, in the course of defending it, my goal is to provide a better theoretical account of biocentric individualism than has been available heretofore. In chapter 2, I provide an original account of the nature and scope of desire in the animal kingdom. I believe this account explains, more clearly than anyone has heretofore, why normal adult mammals and birds are the primary focus of animal rights philosophers and activists. In chapter 3, I improve upon attempts made heretofore to defend the view that even nonconscious organisms, such as plants and "lower animals," have morally considerable interests. And in chapter 4, I develop a novel account, based on Ralph Barton Perry's simple principle of inclusiveness, of how to adjudicate conflicts among competing interests.

So my goal in this book is simultaneously practical and theoretical. I want to effect a rapprochement between animal rights and environmental ethics, and I want in the process to shore up the theoretical underpinnings of biocentric individualism. Accordingly, my intended audience is not only professional philosophers but also activists in the animal rights and environmental movements and scientists, politicians, and policy analysts interested in and affected by those movements. What philosophy can contribute to our understanding of these movements is primarily sustained critical scrutiny of the fundamental concepts and moral reasoning involved; philosophical scrutiny cannot by itself provide us with the last word on the details of environmental policy or our treatment of animals. Many of the conclusions reached in chapters 5 and 6 (and, for that matter, in chapters 2 and 3) are premised on empirical claims, some of which will undoubtedly turn out to be false. I stand ready to be corrected. As a philosopher concerned about our treatment of both animals and the environment, I will feel that I have done enough if I can show that a serious commitment to improving both can spring from the same source.

CHAPTER ONE

A Critique of Environmental Holism

Bотн environmental philosophers and activists commonly claim that we face an "ecological crisis" that will not be solved unless and until a holistic environmental ethic takes hold of our psyches. The search for such an ethic commonly is traced to ecologist Aldo Leopold, who has been called the "patron saint" of environmental ethics. Leopold defined morally right actions as those that "tend to preserve the integrity, stability, and beauty of the biotic community." He stressed that "land ethic . . . implies respect for [one's] fellow members [of the biotic community], and also respect for the community as such." And he characterized such a land ethic as both "an evolutionary possibility and an ecological necessity" (1949, pp. 224–25, 204, 203).

Environmental holism can be either practical or ethical: it is one thing to say that one should take a holistic perspective on the land one manages; it is quite another to say that ecosystems or biotic communities themselves have intrinsic moral value or direct moral standing. Ethical holists attribute intrinsic moral value to ecosystems, or biotic communities, "as such" rather than (or at least in addition to) their individual members, whereas practical holists hold only that it is necessary, in order effectively to manage environmental systems, to view them as complex systems that must be managed as wholes. Bryan Norton has argued convincingly that Leopold was a practical rather than an ethical holist (Norton 1988, 1990, and 1991, chap. 3), but most other authors take him to be an ethical holist, in addition to a practical holist. I will examine the interpretation of Leopold's thought in chapter 6, but for now what I want to emphasize is that Leopold is commonly identified with ethical holism, and it is this kind of holism that I critique in this chapter. I agree that, in developing sound environmental policy, we must focus attention on ecosystems taken as wholes. But this does not imply that we must take ecosystems themselves to be morally considerable. Taking a systems approach to environmental management does not commit one to direct moral consideration for the system as such any more than adopting a systems approach to business management commits one to direct moral consideration of the business as such. A business manager may believe both that ultimately it is only individual wealth that matters and that a business is valuable only as a means to the end of producing individual wealth—and yet still recognize the necessity for managing the business holistically or as a system. Similarly, an environmental manager may believe both that ultimately only individuals' interests count and that an ecosystem is valuable only as a means to satisfying individuals' interests—and yet also recognize the necessity for managing ecosystems holistically or as systems.

To keep from being misunderstood, I will state clearly that, as the argument of chapter 6 will make clear, I am a holist when it comes to designing and implementing environmental policy—that is, I am a practical holist. But, for the reasons given in this chapter, I am not an ethical holist. I do not (or at least I no longer) believe that ecosystems are themselves directly morally considerable. As detailed in the introduction, ethical holism is extremely popular—I would say virtually hegemonic—among self-professed environmentalists and environmental philosophers. But ethical holists bear a large burden of ethical and conceptual proof.

By the ethical burden, I mean the task of showing how we can justify pursuing the goals commonly espoused by environmentalists (population and pollution reduction, wilderness and biodiversity preservation, etc.), and justify these in terms of their effects on ecosystems themselves (rather than in terms of their effects on human beings' long-range interests), without thereby embracing what Tom Regan calls "environmental fascism" (1983, p. 362)—that is, without running roughshod over widely recognized human rights in pursuit of an environmental ideal. I stress that the justification must be in terms of the effects on ecosystems themselves in order to underline the environmental holists' claim that the holistic dimension of their views makes them superior from the point of view of justifying the pursuit of the goals on the environmentalist agenda.

The conceptual burden of proof the holist bears is to explain how a system as such can be conceived of as having intrinsic value. The paradigm example of an entity with intrinsic value, with direct moral standing, is a normal adult human being. This is the usual starting point of discussions in ethics, and with good reason: a view in which intrinsic value was not ascribed to the satisfaction of at least some human interests would be prima facie highly implausible. Ethical holists must either (1) explain how a very different kind of entity—an ecosystem—can have interests or (2) defend a different basis for the ascription of intrinsic value and show that ecosystems meet this criterion.

In this chapter, I describe in greater detail the conceptual challenges faced by supporters of the holistic approach to environmental ethics. I do not think that any available approach adequately meets these burdens. Showing that no currently available version of environmental holism meets these burdens of proof would not invalidate the whole approach, but a detailed account of the burdens serves as a brief for individualism; the object is to convince the reader that the individualistic approach to environmental ethics deserves another look. Those who are already convinced of this could skip to the conclusion of this chapter, but, given how hegemonic holism has become among environmental ethicists, it is important to spend some time detailing the problems a truly holistic view faces.

I will focus primarily on the views of J. Baird Callicott, for several reasons. First, Callicott has emerged as the leading philosophical interpreter of Leopold's widely influential land ethic. Second, Callicott's work is in two ways paradigmatic of the holistic tradition in environmental ethics. He effectively identifies environmental ethics with holism by characterizing the holistic Leopold land ethic as "the exemplary type" in an ostensive definition of environmental ethics (1980, p. 311). And Callicott explicitly claims that the holistic dimension of the Leopold land ethic is what makes it an appropriate ethical foundation for sound environmental policy. There is, he says, "an intolerable contradiction" between individualistic views in which, like anthropocentrism and animal rights views, intrinsic value is attributed only to individuals and holistic views like the land ethic, because the welfare of a "community as such" is not reducible to the aggregate welfare of its members, and sound environmental policy often runs counter to the welfare of human beings and various other individuals (1980, esp. pp. 323–24 and 327–29).[1] Finally, although Callicott's reading of the Leopold land ethic fits most naturally with the view that ecosystems themselves have interests, he explicitly denies that they do, so a thorough discussion of his views provides occasion for criticism of both approaches to environmental holism: those in which interests are attributed to ecosystems and those in which they are not.

CALLICOTT'S INTERPRETATION OF LEOPOLD'S HOLISM

In a series of articles, Callicott has argued that the land ethic grew from philosophically respectable roots when Leopold followed Charles Darwin to combine "a Humean-Smithian moral psychology" with modern ecological and evolutionary science. Both David Hume and Adam Smith explain moral phenomena—the moral judgments we actually make, our tendencies to condemn certain things and to praise others in moral terms—via the operation of natural sentiments, most notably sympathy, for the fellow members of the communities in which we live. Callicott agrees: "The scope and specific content of ethics will reflect both the perceived boundaries and actual structure or organization of a cooperative community or society. *Ethics and society or community are correlative*" (1987, p. 191). Callicott then argues that ecological and evolutionary science has trans-

---

1. Callicott has since refined some of what he said in his 1980 "Triangular Affair" paper, but he still maintains that individualism is opposed to sound environmental policy. See, for example, Callicott 1986 and 1994.

formed our conception of community in such a way that we (or at least the evolutionarily and ecologically literate among us) can perceive every other living thing as a member of a common biotic community to which our natural sentiments therefore extend.

If Callicott is correct that the land ethic's holism is what makes it an appropirate ethical foundation for sound environmental policy, then the viability of the Leopold land ethic hinges crucially on the following question. Do the moral sentiments of an evolutionarily and ecologically literate individual extend only to the fellow members of his or her biotic community or also to the community as such? Only insofar as it implies respect for the community "as such"—as opposed to respect for individual members of the community—is the land ethic truly holistic.

No Sympathy for Systems

Callicott explicitly maintains that it is his Humean–Smithian moral psychology that, in light of Darwinian theory, makes respect for a community as such possible:

> Respect for wholes, for the community as such and its various subsystems, is a theoretical possibility for the land ethic because it is conceptually and historically related to the Humean–Darwinian theoretical complex. Both individual members of society and the community as such, the social whole, . . . are the objects of certain special, naturally selected moral sentiments. (1986, p. 408)

Callicott compares the sentiment that the ecologically literate individual feels toward his or her biotic community to the sentiments of loyalty or patriotism.

Callicott's reconstruction of the land ethic's philosophical foundations fits Leopold's text nicely. It illuminates Leopold's claims that the land ethic is both "an evolutionary possibility and an ecological necessity" (1949, p. 203), and it fits perfectly with his characterization of people as "plain members and *citizens* of the biotic community" (p. 204, emphasis added). So if a nonreductive account of something like patriotism can meaningfully be applied to biotic communities, then Callicott's reconstruction provides the land ethic with deep roots in Western moral philosophy.

The account must be nonreductive, however, because a reductive account (that equates the ecosystem's welfare with the aggregate or average[2] welfare of its individual members) would not be truly holistic. Just as someone who takes a systems approach to managing a complex system is not committed to the system as such having any moral standing, a thinker who attributes direct moral standing

2. I say "aggregate or average," because there are more ways to aggregate the happiness of many individuals than by simply averaging.

only to sentient organisms (a sentientist such as Peter Singer, for example) can speak quite meaningfully of a community's welfare without implying that the community as such has a welfare. A sentientist measures community welfare by aggregating or averaging the welfare of the individuals in it and could adapt such an approach to ecosystems without embracing holism. But Callicott's claim is that ethical support for sound environmental policy comes from a truly holistic view that the system as such has direct moral standing.

Both Hume and Smith describe the sentiment of sympathy, which plays a central role in their thinking, as operating exclusively toward other individuals rather than toward the community as such. These authors sometimes write as if a community has a good of its own. For instance, Hume often refers to "the interests of society" or "the happiness of society" (1957 [1751], p. 47), and Smith at one point observes that

> The state or sovereignty in which we have been born and educated, and under the protection of which we continue to live, is, in ordinary cases, the greatest society upon whose happiness or misery, our good or bad conduct can have much influence. (1976 [1759], p. 227)

Such ways of speaking could be taken to suggest that Hume and Smith believe that a society can itself be an object of concern, that a society can have interests or a welfare that is not reducible to that of its individual members, and that it is possible to act out of sympathy for a community as such. But these ways of speaking are misleading. For both Hume and Smith, we are capable of sympathizing only with individuals. The reason is that, for both authors, what we identify with is other individuals' passions. (Today, instead of talking about their passions, we would more naturally speak of other persons' feelings, emotions, wants, or desires.) Because a society or community is not itself conscious, a society or community cannot literally be said to have any passions with which one could identify. So for Hume and Smith, as for any sentientist, talk of the "welfare of the community" is a shorthand way of referring to the aggregate or average happiness of the individuals who make up society.

Darwin too sometimes speaks as if the welfare of the community as such is the object of human sympathy, but, as I show in the remainder of this subsection, these remarks are shorthand for more complicated statements about the welfare of individuals. My point is not that Darwin denies that group selection accounts for the emergence of the moral sense in human beings. In the remainder of this subsection, I ask a question about what kind of moral sense Darwin thinks evolution has produced in humans. My point is that Darwin thinks group selection occurs because groups of humans who sympathize with other individual humans in their group have a selective advantage over groups of humans who lack this sympathy with other individuals in their own groups rather than because groups of humans who feel sympathy for their group as such (or some analog like patriotism) have a selective advantage. The claim that group selection drove the evolution of the moral sentiment does not imply that the moral sentiment is holistic rather than individualistic, and, insofar as Darwin followed Hume and Smith, the moral sentiment is individualistic.

In an early chapter of *The Descent of Man*, Darwin adopts Smith's and Hume's terminology, citing their works and asserting that "the moral sense or conscience is by far the most important . . . of all the differences between man and the lower animals" (1874, p. 112). In discussing the moral sense's operation, he sometimes speaks of "the wishes of the community" and "the public good," and he describes the sense as a specifically "*social* sense" (p. 114). But, as I have just shown, neither Hume nor Smith believes that sympathy for a community as such is possible, and thus, in adopting their terminology, Darwin implicitly adopts their individualistic stance.

In "Conceptual Foundations of the Land Ethic," Callicott (1986, p. 405) quotes from the conclusion of a section in *The Descent of Man* in which Darwin argues that "the strictly social virtues"—such things as truthfulness, obedience, and tendencies away from murder, robbery, and treachery—must have emerged first, because these are the "virtues which must be practised, at least generally, by rude men, so that they may associate in a body." The "self-regarding virtues," such things as temperance and "female virtue," are of relatively recent origin (1874, pp. 132–34). Darwin concludes that

> actions are regarded by savages, and were probably so regarded by primeval man, as good or bad, solely as they obviously affect the welfare of the tribe— not that of the species, nor that of an individual member of the tribe. This conclusion agrees well with the belief that the so-called moral sense is aborigi- nally derived from the social instincts, for both relate at first exclusively to the community. (p. 134)

In this passage, Darwin clearly does distinguish between "the welfare of the tribe" and that of "an individual member," and he clearly does say that "savages" evaluate actions in terms of the latter rather than the former. But just afterward, Darwin gives an explicitly reductive definition of "the general good": "The term, the general good, may be defined as the rearing of the greatest number of indi- viduals in full vigor and health, with all their faculties perfect, under the condi- tions to which they are subjected" (p. 136). Are these passages inconsistent? Not at all. Notice that, in the passage quoted by Callicott, Darwin draws a distinction between "the welfare of the tribe" and that of "*an* individual member," not between "the welfare of the tribe" and "the welfare of its individual members." Nothing in the section from which Callicott quotes implies that, according to Darwin, a community as such has a welfare that is not somehow reducible to the welfare of its individual members. In that section, Darwin's concern is simply to show that the first virtues to emerge were virtues because they contributed to the welfare of the community—however that welfare is defined—rather than because they contributed to the welfare of an individual who practiced them.

Like Hume and Smith's talk about the happiness of society, then, Darwin's comments about "the wishes of the community" and "the public good" are a shorthand for detailed comments about the wishes or good of individuals who make up the community or public. So, *pace* Callicott, there seems to be no historical antecedent of holism in the writings of Hume, Smith, or Darwin.

To his credit, Callicott does not attribute to Hume, Smith, and Darwin the view that we are capable of sympathizing with a community as such. Callicott compares the sentiment that ecologically literate individuals feel toward their biotic communities to patriotism. But for Hume, Smith, and Darwin, patriotism without sympathy is empty. Sympathy is such an important sentiment in the writings of Hume and Smith not only because it tells us something about the motives of a moral agent but also, and crucially, because it suggests a convenient way in which a moral agent can come to understand what is good and bad for another individual. Loyalty and patriotism describe the motives of an agent but without suggesting how the agent knows what would be good for the object of his loyalty and patriotism. For people feeling something like loyalty or patriotism to have any clue how to treat their biotic communities, they need a criterion of ecosystemic health or welfare, but Humean–Smithian moral psychology provides only the kind of reductive account of ecosystemic welfare that Callicott claims is environmentally inadequate. Callicott insists that ecosystemic well-being not be assessed reductively, in terms of the well-being of its individual members, let alone in terms of a rather small subset of them (the sentient ones).

Organicism and the Concept of Land Health

But Callicott does not claim that Leopold lifted the land ethic ready-made from the pages of these authors with all of their philosophical baggage in tow. He claims only that their views "informed Leopold's thinking in the late 1940's" (1987, p. 189). Given that Leopold frequently described land as "a collective organism" that can be "healthy or unhealthy" (e.g., 1949, pp. 221–23, and 1991b and 1991c), he may have had a broader, less psychologistic understanding of welfare that can be applied both to an individual organism (whether conscious or nonconscious) and to a "community as such." In chapter 3, I argue that a nonarbitrary and nontrivial criterion of organismic welfare can be derived from study of the biological functions of an organism's component organs and sub-systems. So I agree that, if ecosystems literally were organisms, then we could plausibly speak of conditions being better and worse for them and that we could do this without attributing psychological states to them.

In the 1930s, when Leopold began writing the essays that became *A Sand County Almanac*, plant successionist Frederick Clements and his followers were still touting an organismic conception of ecosystems. However, in two articles published in 1920 and 1935 (the latter being the article in which he introduces the term "ecosystem"), Arthur G. Tansley gives the classic criticism of Clements's literal organicism. Tansley argues that, while ecosystems are sufficiently analogous to organisms to be called "quasi-organisms," the disanalogies show that ecosystems are not organisms in any literal sense. In particular, Tansley stresses that, unlike the organs of a body, individual organisms from a given ecosystem are capable of existing independently of each other. From this "general independence" of an ecosystem's constituent organisms follow two other disanalogies between an ecosystem and an organism: (1) ecosystems lack "the physical unity and definiteness of outline" characteristic of an organism and (2) an ecosystem's organisms can "transfer themselves to another community and become true members of it," an ability with no significant analog in an organism's organs. (See Tansley 1920, at pp. 122–26, and 1935, esp. pp. 289–92.)

Leopold surely knew of Tansley's criticism of Clements, although he appears to have corresponded only minimally with Clements and perhaps not at all with Tansley (Meine 1988, p. 564, n. 54, and pp. 635–36 [Tansley's name is not in the index]). Why the organismic language survived in "The Land Ethic" is therefore something of a mystery. In two essays (1990, 1992), Callicott admits that the "concept of ecosystem health is metaphorical," and yet he states that the key philosophical problem for the land ethic is the question of the soundness of that metaphor: "To what extent," he asks, "are ecosystems analogous to organisms, and to what extent therefore can we speak intelligibly of land health?" As Callicott points out, "bodily health is a paradigm case of something that is intrinsically as well as instrumentally valuable; it is good in and of itself, as well as a necessary condition for getting on with our projects" (1990, p. 231). As chapter 3 attests, I agree wholeheartedly. But, when applied to ecosystems, the "health" in "bodily health" is metaphorical. When teaching ethics, one can use an equally apt metaphor by describing utilitarians as thinking that people are "cups" that contain greater or lesser amounts of positive or negative utility, but the aptness of this metaphor does not make it the case that one can drink coffee from a person. Similarly, the aptness of the bodily health metaphor in describing the views of ethical holists does not by itself make it the case that ecosystems are directly morally considerable. The question is not, "Can ecosystems be described metaphorically as organisms?" but rather, "Are the specific literal analogies that can be drawn between organisms and ecosystems analogies that make it plausible to say that ecosystems are directly morally considerable?"

The only literal analogy Callicott draws is this:

Ecosystems and organisms . . . have one very fundamental, not to say essential, characteristic in common: the capacity for self-renewal. More technically expressed, organisms and ecosystems are both autopoietic: self-organizing and self-recreating. (1992, p. 51)

But surely the capacity for self-renewal does not by itself make an ecosystem directly morally considerable. Any system that exhibits self-organized criticality— sand heaps are a classic example (Bak and Chen 1991)—is self-renewing in much the same sense as is an ecosystem. Growing sand heaps receive outside inputs (in the field, grains arrive wind blown; in experiments with or models of self-organized criticality, grains are dropped slowly onto the peak), but so do eco-systems (solar energy arrives, weather patterns move over, and organisms im-migrate and emigrate). We need to know more about what is being renewed before we can say that the capacity for self-renewal is morally significant.

An obvious place to start is with the "integrity, stability, and beauty of the biotic community" to which Leopold refers in his summary statement of the land ethic. Leopold apparently believes that the three go together, that, if the integrity of an ecosystem is maintained, then it will be both stable and beautiful. But even if an ecosystem's welfare could plausibly be said to consist in its integrity and stability, surely it cannot consist in its beauty. Beauty may be intrinsically valu-able, and it may even be an inevitable accompaniment of health, but an organ-ism's (or ecosystem's) beauty is not constitutive of its good. Only insofar as one's beauty allows one more effectively to satisfy one's interests does one's beauty contribute to one's welfare. But this is an instrumental rather than constitutive contribution. This is all the more evident in the case of an ecosystem. Even if an aesthetic appreciation of ecosystems unfailingly accompanies a purely cognitive understanding of their origins and structure, the aesthetic response is not con-stitutive of their welfare; at most, it contributes to ours. It accompanies our understanding of their welfare, which must in turn consist in something else.

What then of integrity and stability? It is impossible adequately to evaluate these terms' application to ecosystems without first being more specific about what is meant by the words "ecosystem" and "biotic community." Although Leopold uses the terms interchangeably, contemporary ecologists usually draw one explicit distinction between the two. "Ecosystem" usually is used to refer to both the biotic and abiotic components of an ecological system. "Biotic com-munity," by contrast, is used to refer solely to the biotic components, specifically to the interrelated populations of organisms that make up an ecosystem at a given time. Consider these typical examples of biotic communities: (1) an upper Mid-western prairie community, (2) a pioneer community of lodgepole pine in the Rockies, (3) a piñon-juniper community on a mountainside in southern Arizona, and (4) a beech and maple community in a Southern bottomland. Each is a constellation of species populations that exists on a given piece of land for only a limited period of time. This is obvious in the case of the prairie and the lod-gepole pine community, which, if they last for more than a few generations, are maintained by allogenic forces (e.g., fire). In the absence of fire, the prairie will soon be replaced by an oak woodland, and the lodgepoles will soon be replaced by fir and hemlock. However, on a large enough time scale, every plant community is transient. As the climate changes, a piñon-juniper community will be replaced by a forest of either saguaro cacti or ponderosa pine (depending on which direction the climate shifts), and, as drainage patterns dry out the soil around them, beech and maple trees growing in a Southern bottomland will be replaced by oak. The significance of this is the following.

Some ecologists draw (either explicitly or implicitly) a second and, for our purposes, a more important distinction between "biotic community" and "ecosystem." For example, Eugene Odum, in his classic textbook *Basic Ecology* (1983), devotes an entire chapter to "Development and Evolution in the Ecosystem." The topic, of course, is the familiar concept of succession. But the title of Odum's chapter dramatizes an important point. If "ecosystem" is used analogously with "biotic community," and a biotic community is identified with a specific constellation of species populations, then by definition succession cannot occur "in an ecosystem." Only if "ecosystem" is taken to mean the systematic succession of biotic communities across a landscape can an ecosystem be said to "evolve" via succession. An ecosystem "develops" or "evolves" as various biotic communities come and go within it.

This discussion of definitions is directly relevant to the question of whether or not integrity and stability can be made into useful criteria of ecosystem welfare. If "ecosystem" is used to mean "biotic community," then, so long as it exists, an ecosystem cannot fail to exhibit integrity and stability. A given biotic community goes out of existence as soon as its keystone species disappears or various species' connections are sufficiently diminished. To recommend integrity and stability as criteria for assessing the health of a biotic community is like recommending presence of brain activity as a criterion of human health. Certainly when brain activity ceases, a human being has been harmed, but the criterion is much too coarse grained: it identifies harm with death. Integrity and stability are all but useless as indicators of a biotic community's health. They are criteria for the individuation of biotic communities, but as such they are all or nothing. They do not allow us to discriminate usefully between what is and is not good, between what is good and what is better, for a biotic community as such.[3]

3. Note that Callicott favors the term "biocoenosis" over either "biotic community" or "ecosystem." This term is relatively unfamiliar to American, British, and Australasian readers, although it is commonly used in the European and Russian literatures, where it is used synonymously with "biotic community." The term is formed from the conjunction of Greek terms for life (*bi*) and sharing or having in common (*koinosis*). Thus it means, literally, living things functioning together (*Webster's Third International Dictionary* and Odum 1983, p. 4). Callicott presumably prefers "biocoenosis" to "ecosystem," because sympathy, loyalty, and patriotism sound more at home in a "community" than in a "system"; and presumably he prefers "biocoenosis" to "biotic community," because the former's etymology stresses interdependence and cooperation. However, the fact that Callicott's favored term "biocoenosis" is etymologically closer to "biotic community" than it

Furthermore, if "ecosystem" is used to mean "biotic community," then eco-systems cannot be said to evolve or develop in significant ways. As ponderosas replace piñons on a mountainside, there is no one biotic community that is changing; one is going out of existence and another is coming into existence. Natural succession cannot occur within a biotic community; it occurs within an ecosystem when various biotic communities replace one another through time. Presumably, Callicott believes that natural succession is a good thing, but his apparent identification of "ecosystem" with "biotic community" does not allow him to say that it is good for a biotic community as such. It might still be good for us or other organisms, but it cannot be good for the biotic community as such, which goes out of existence in the process.

What of the integrity and stability of ecosystems, as opposed to biotic com-munities? Leopold speculates that an ecosystem's stability depends upon its in-tegrity, and he appears to believe that, with some notable exceptions, the original, naturally evolved ecosystem is the most stable and fecund that can be achieved on the land (1949, pp. 210 and 218–19).[4] So by the "integrity" of an ecosystem he could mean being "complete" or "entire"—that is, "retaining the full com-plement of indigenous species." Surely, though, this is too strong a notion of integrity on which to hang the notion of ecosystem health. An ecosystem can remain stable and fecund while undergoing a complete change in the species populations that make it up, as when a piñon-juniper woodland is replaced by a pine forest.

Leopold knows this, and he even recognizes that in some places dramatic anthropogenic changes occurred without destroying the land's stability and fe-cundity:

> Biota seem to differ in their capacity to sustain violence. Western Europe, for example, carries a far different pyramid than Caesar found there. Some large animals are lost; many new plants and animals are introduced, some of which escape as pests; the remaining natives are greatly changed in distribution and abundance. Yet the soil is still fertile, the waters flow normally, the new structure seems to function and to persist. There is no visible stoppage of the circuit. (1991a, p. 270)

Consequently, Callicott suggests that by "integrity" Leopold means something more like "retains the capacity for self-renewal," and he suggests that both "natural" and anthropogenic changes can be evaluated by this same criterion (1992, pp. 46–47). Following Leopold, he argues that, while ecology remains

---

is to "ecosystem" is a distinct philosophical liability, given these remarks on the distinction between the latter two terms.

4. This point is developed further in chapter 6 of the present work.

"[in]capable of specifying the norms of land health," "the 'symptoms' of 'land-sickness' " are already well known:

> soil erosion and loss of fertility, hydrologic abnormalities, and the occasional irruptions of some species and the mysterious local extinctions of others, . . . qualitative deterioration in farm and forest products, the outbreak of pests and disease epidemics, and boom and bust wildlife population cycles. (pp. 48, 50)

As a criterion of ecosystem health, this account of "integrity" fares better than integrity and stability as indicators of the health of a biotic community as such. It certainly is possible for a system to possess the capacity for self-renewal to a greater or lesser degree, and it is plausible to say that some or all of the "symptoms of land illness" to which Callicott refers are indicators of low capacity for self-renewal. Here, however, we come back to a problem discussed earlier. If the "health" of an ecosystem consists in its capacity for self-renewal, and a broad range of things (including sand heaps) have the capacity for self-renewal, why should we think that the "health" of an ecosystem is really health, in any morally significant sense? Obviously, if we value ecosystems for certain services they provide, then the capacity for self-renewal is instrumentally valuable. However, Callicott's claim is that ecosystems carry intrinsic value, not just instrumental value, and it is not clear why the capacity for self-renewal would by itself carry intrinsic value.

The development of a nonreductive and nonarbitrary concept of land health is crucial to the success of Callicott's philosophical project. Grounding the Leopold land ethic on a Humean–Smithian moral psychology seems most likely to succeed either (1) by showing that ecosystems themselves have interests or (2) by embracing a reductive account of ecosystem health. Callicott consistently seeks to distance himself from conativist, "extensionist" views, so he himself is skeptical of the first tack (note that the title of his own essay on ecosystem health is "Aldo Leopold's Metaphor"). But in terms of its support for the environmentalist agenda, Callicott insists that it is the *holism* of the land ethic that makes it superior, so he refuses to take the second tack.

OTHER DEFENSES OF ETHICAL HOLISM

I conclude this critique by briefly considering several other defenses of environmental holism, defenses that begin neither from Humean–Smithian moral psychology nor from claims about the health or welfare of the system as such.

In *Foundations of Environmental Ethics* (1989), Eugene C. Hargrove argues that naturally evolving ecosystems have a special kind of beauty and (following G. E. Moore) that moral agents have prima facie duties to protect and promote the existence of such beauty in the world. However, given the centrality of the duties of beneficience and nonmaleficence to our shared conception of morality, it is difficult to see how these prima facie duties could override duties generated by the existence of interests. For example, an attempt to justify a ban on logging in the Pacific Northwest's remaining old-growth forests solely in terms of these forests' special beauty would be on very shaky ground if the ban would cause economic dislocation of thousands of loggers and mill workers. If in response it is claimed (as it commonly is) that present logging practices are ultimately un-sustainable and that old growth can be preserved if the practices are abandoned now rather than later, then the aesthetic argument does have more force. But what makes the augmented argument sound more plausible is the individualistic (and anthropocentric) consideration that individual loggers' interests will be sim-ilarly adversely affected whether we stop logging now or later. It is only in this context (i.e., other things being equal) that the aesthetic considerations seem compelling. So an aesthetic approach such as Hargrove's, although holistic, does not promise to justify the kinds of policies that are on the environmentalist agenda.

In *Environmental Ethics: Duties to and Values in the Natural World* (1988), Holmes Rolston III maintains that only higher animals have "psychological in-terests" and that only individual organisms can literally be said to be healthy or diseased (pp. 52, 97). On his view, ecosystems as such have no interests or a good of their own that would give them direct moral standing. Yet he insists that they have more than instrumental value, because they produce organisms, which do have intrinsic value. In a typical passage, he writes:

> We confront a *projective nature*, one restlessly full of projects—stars, comets, planets, moons, and also rocks, crystals, rivers, canyons, seas. The life in which these astronomical and geological processes culminate is still more impressive, but it is of a piece with the whole projective system. . . . The system is of value for its capacity to throw forward (pro-ject [*sic*]) all the storied natural history. On that scale humans come late and it seems shortsighted and arrogant for such latecomers to say that the system is only of instrumental value for humans. (pp. 197–98)

Rolston coins a new term for this special value—"systemic value"—insisting that it is not the same as intrinsic value, which only organisms have.[5]

Although I have trouble understanding precisely what Rolston means by "systemic value" and how it differs from intrinsic value, it does seem clear that, in the argument quoted above, Rolston commits a species of the genetic fallacy,

---

5. "We might say that the system itself has intrinsic value; it is, after all, the womb of life. Yet again, the 'loose' system, though it has value *in* itself, does not seem to have any value *for* itself, as organisms do seem to have. It is not a value owner, though it is a value producer. It is not a value beholder; it is a value holder in the sense that it projects, conserves, elaborates value holders (organisms)" (Rolston, 1988, p. 187).

specifically the fallacy of assuming that because X came from (had its genesis in) Y, if X has value then Y, which produced X, has value of a similar kind. That is, Rolston's argument appears to be that ecosystems have more than instrumental value because their products have more than instrumental value. But surely this is fallacious. Suppose that an otherwise devastating hurricane happens to clear up the waters of a lagoon so that it is very beautiful or that air pollution happens to create more beautiful sunsets. Just because the lagoon or the sunsets have more than purely instrumental value, it does not follow that the hurricane and the pollution also have more than purely instrumental value. It would not be fallacious to argue that, because X came from Y, if X has value of a certain kind, then Y has instrumental value (as a source of that value), but it is fallacious to argue that, because X came from Y and Y has intrinsic value, Y must also have intrinsic value or even a value more like intrinsic value than purely instrumental value.

Rolston does offer the following reason for thinking that "instrumental value" fails accurately to describe the value in question:

> Member components serve the system, as when warblers regulate insect popu-lations; perhaps that is systemic instrumental value. But—if we reconsider this terminology—the decentered sytem, despite its successions and headings, has no integrated program, nothing it is defending, and to say that an ecosytem makes instrumental use of warblers to regulate insect populations seems awk-ward. (1988, p. 187)

Of course it seems awkward to say that an ecosystem "*makes* instrumental use of warblers," because ecosystems have no intentions (no "integrated program"). It would be equally awkward to say that a hammer makes instrumental use of nails in building a house. But no such thing is implied when I say that an eco-system (or a population of warblers) is of (or has) instrumental value. When I say that an ecosystem is instrumentally valuable (or has instrumental value) be-cause it produces organisms with intrinsic value, I do not attribute any intentions to the system. This is no more strange than saying that a hammer is instrumen-tally valuable (or has instrumental value) because it can be used (along with nails) to produce a house.

In *Environmental Justice* (1988), Peter Wenz deploys an argument similar to Rolston's and then gives a response to the objection that it commits the genetic fallacy. Wenz appeals to the "common-sense conservative principle" that "One should not interfere with what is working well," and then he observes that

> if human beings are so extraordinarily wonderful, then the evolutionary pro-cesses which produced them must have worked well. It follows ... that we should not interfere with evolutionary processes ... [and] we should protect wilderness areas, where those processes are best preserved. (p. 300)

Wenz then anticipates the response I just made to such arguments. He compares my response to that of someone who attributes to a train only the instrumental value of getting its passengers to their destinations:

> The objector's reasoning ignores the arguments for animal rights, for kindness toward animals, and for respecting every living thing . . . [and] simply assumes, without justification, that human beings are alone of inherent worth, and this is unacceptable. Reverting to the analogy of the train, when we do not know whom to count as a potential passenger, we cannot say when the train has transported all concerned to their destination, nor whether the train will be needed in the future. Under such conditions of ignorance, it is reasonable to continue to value the train *for its (largely unknown) potential service.* (p. 301, emphasis altered)

This reply is unconvincing, however, for the following reason. Although earlier in the book Wenz repeats the nostrum that individualistic theories lead to environmentally unsound consequences specifically because they include "no *direct concern* for the state of many environmental constituents, such as trees, species of plants and animals, mountains, lakes, rivers, and soils" (pp. 208–9)[6] (I would say that he writes as if practical holism implied ethical holism), in his response to my objection Wenz does not claim to establish that ecosystems have intrinsic value. Wenz claims only that, if the individual organisms that are the products of evolution have "inherent worth" (which is the term he opposes to "instrumental value"), then we should continue to value naturally evolving ecosystems for their "(largely unknown) potential service" (i.e., instrumentally). This is not a fallacious argument, but it establishes only that ecosystems are indirectly morally considerable—that is, by virtue of their relationship to what is directly morally considerable, namely individual living organisms.

CONCLUSION

In conclusion, let me emphasize again that I am not a foe of conservation, I do not oppose efforts to preserve endangered species and ecosystems, and I do not hanker to see remaining wild places covered with strip malls and urbane sprawl. On the contrary, my intuitive judgment is that we ought to give back much of the earth to its wild, nonhuman inhabitants. As a philosopher, I insist only that we be clear about our reasons for doing so. At the beginning of my career, I was tempted by ethical holism, because I too thought that the environmental crisis would be solved only once a holistic ethic took hold of our psyches—I too tended

6. This statement is made about utilitarianism specifically, but Wenz finds the same problem in human rights theories, animal rights theories, and Rawls's account of distributive justice (1988, p. 250).

to think that practical holism implies ethical holism (Varner 1985, 1987). But, as I argue in this chapter, holism faces an enormous burden of proof, one that available versions of the view fail to meet.

I conclude that biocentric individualism deserves another look. In the following three chapters, I develop a version of this view rooted in an analysis of interests as the core ethical concept. Because the concepts of beneficence and nonmaleficence are so central to our thinking about ethics, it is crucially important to understand which beings have interests. This is because to have interests in a morally relevant sense is to have a good or a welfare of one's own, which can be positively or adversely affected by the actions of moral agents.

CHAPTER TWO

Localizing Desire

WHAT THINGS do have interests? The paradigm case of an interested being is a desiring creature. Not everything that is in one's interests is something one desires. A smoker may recognize that quitting is ultimately in his best interests and yet desire another cigarette more strongly than anything else. But it is at least true that, as William James puts it, any "demand" ought, "for its own sole sake, to be satisfied," that a desire "*makes* itself valid by the fact that it exists at all" (1948, p. 73). Taken in isolation, every desire defines an interest of the creature with that desire.[1] And so it is important to ask, "Which creatures have desires?" The scope of interests in nonhuman nature will be at least as large as the scope of desire.

Desire is a familiar and important concept in many facets of our lives. We find it very useful to describe persons' actions in terms of what desires they express, are motivated by, or are designed to satisfy. For instance, telling you that "John is looking for some microbrewery beer" is far more informative and potentially useful to you than describing the particular physical movements he is performing (walking into liquor stores, scanning the shelves, and so on). We also attribute desires to companion animals. Telling you that "Nanci wants to get a toy out from behind the stove" is much more informative and potentially useful to you than saying that the cat is nosing about and scratching in certain ways. Even behavioristically inclined scientists have acknowledged this. Primate researcher D. O. Hebb once observed:

> Whatever the anthropomorphic terminology may seem to imply about conscious states in the chimpanzee, it provides an intelligible and practical guide to behavior . . . [it points to] some order, or relationship between isolated acts that is essential to comprehension of the behavior. (1946, p. 88, emphasis removed)

1. In chapter 4, I reply to the objection that this is not true of some desires, like a desire to rape.

We often go overboard in attributing desires to nonhuman animals. However much it may amuse us, telling you that "Nanci wishes Herzog had stayed with the Cardinals" will not help you understand the cat's behavior. Here a desire is attributed to an animal that can plausibly be said to have some desires but not plausibly this desire. Other times, however, desire attributions are very useful for understanding entities that, when we are speaking more carefully, we would want to deny have any desires at all. For example, evolutionary biologists commonly describe species as "trying out new adaptations." In his classic book on octopi, for example, M. J. Wells described an evolutionary change in the shell morphology of the octopods' ancestors thus: "A likely interpretation is that this represents a series of attempts to shore up an otherwise rather fragile envelope against increasing pressure" (1978, p. 6). The pressure increased over generations as these mollusks lived in progressively deeper waters. Now no octopod ever "attempted" to make the shells stronger. And while readily using such language and acknowledging its usefulness, no evolutionary biologist believes that species of organisms "really" desire anything. Such uses of "desire" are purely heuristic.

How do we separate the "real" uses from such purely heuristic uses? Where in the phylogenetic scale do "real" desires fade into purely metaphorical ones? To answer this question, I now examine more precisely what "desire" means in its nonmetaphorical use and then show what the behavioral and physiological evidence suggests about the presence of desires, so construed, in various nonhuman animals.

THE CORE CONCEPT OF DESIRE

By "desire," I actually mean a whole cluster of similar concepts, as both James's habit of speaking interchangeably of "desires" and "demands" and my own choice of examples in the introductory section indicate. One can indicate what one's desires are by saying what one demands, what one wants or wishes, what one needs, what one is trying to do, what one is looking for, what one's intention is, and so on.

There are, of course, some differences. For example, wants are contrasted with needs in terms of their seriousness, whereas desires can be either trivial or serious. Again, "intention," "trying," and "demanding" all suggest conscious planning more definitely than either "wants," "needs," or "desires," which we sometimes speak of as blindly impelling us. And G. E. M. Anscombe observes that the "primitive sign of wanting is [actually] *trying to get*" (1963, sec. 36), but, as Aristotle observes, we often wish for what we know it is beyond our power to achieve (*Nicomachean Ethics*, 1111b20–30), as our word "vellicity," often defined as "the lowest form of desire," also indicates.

Despite such important differences, however, all these concepts are related to one another insofar as each of them, in at least one identifiable usage, expresses the same thing. This core concept—variously expressed in the language of intentions, wants, wishes, needs, and desires—is my subject here, and henceforth, when I speak of "desires," I intend what I say to apply also to "wants," "wishes," "needs," and "intentions" when these terms are used in this core sense.

I suggest that in this core sense a sentence of the form "*A* desires *X*" is true if and only if:

(1) *A* is disposed to pursue *X*;
(2) *A* pursues *X* in the way he, she, or it does because *A* previously engaged or concurrently engages in practical reasoning about how to achieve *X* or objects like *X*, where engaging in practical reasoning includes both drawing inferences from beliefs of the form "*Y* is a means to *X*" and the hypothesis formation and testing by which such beliefs are acquired and revised; and
(3) this practical reasoning is at least potentially conscious.

This is not obviously the set of necessary and jointly sufficient conditions we place on "real" desire attributions in day-to-day life. However, I think it an acceptable set of conditions in philosophical contexts, for three reasons.

First, this set of conditions can be used in several ways to explain why the evolutionary biologists' use of "desire" in describing the evolution of species is heuristic rather than "real." On the assumption that evolutionary adaptation occurs at the level of individuals, one must conclude that a species' evolution is a side effect rather than a goal of any relevant entity. So species do not "really" have desires, because they are not "really" goal directed (condition 1). Similarly, on the assumption that consciousness requires something functionally similar to an animal nervous system, one must conclude that species do not "really" have desires because they are not potentially conscious (condition 3). This is also why all attributions of desires to plants are metaphorical. Also, it is not cogent to say that random mutation under selection pressures "really" constitutes "hypothesis formation and testing" (condition 2).

My second reason is that the above definition or something very close to it has been widely accepted by the principals on either side of the animal rights debate (e.g., Regan 1983, pp. 84–84 and 243; Frey 1980, p. 55), as well as by authors writing on nonapplied topics (Anscombe 1963, secs. 22, 36, and 41). Here I limit myself to one example. In a seminal passage from "The Rights of Animals and Unborn Generations," Joel Feinberg writes:

> A desiring creature may want *X* because he seeks anything that is φ, and *X* appears to be φ to him; or he may be seeking *Y*, and he believes, or expects, or hopes that *X* will be a means to *Y*. If he desires *X* in order to get *Y*, this implies that he believes that *X* will bring *Y* about, or at least that he has some sort of

brute expectation that is a primitive correlate of belief. But what of the desire for φ (or for *Y*) itself? Perhaps a creature has such a "desire" as an ultimate set, as if he had come into existence all "wound up" to pursue φ-ness or *Y*-ness, and his is not to reason why. Such a propensity, I think, would not qualify as a desire. Mere brute longings unmediated by beliefs—longings for one knows not what—might perhaps be a primitive form of consciousness (I don't want to beg that question) but they are altogether different from the sort of thing we mean by "desire" . . . [I]f desires or wants are the materials interests are made of, mindless creatures have no interests of their own. (1974, pp. 52–53)

Feinberg agrees that to have a desire is to be disposed to pursue a goal. Feinberg also contrasts a desire with a "mere brute longing" in terms of the former's (1) being mediated by beliefs and (2) involving reasoning, and he takes desire to involve practical reasoning utilizing beliefs of the form "*Y* is a means to *X*." Finally, Feinberg contrasts creatures who have desires with "mindless creatures," he contrasts desires with a "[more] primitive form of consciousness." Feinberg's characterization thus closely parallels the above definition of desiring behavior.

There are some subtle and important differences, however. The conscious reflection that accompanies desiring behavior involves hypothesis formation and testing more often than it does the drawing of inferences from one's beliefs. Rarely do we consciously entertain the major and minor premises of an Aristotelian practical syllogism, "cold beer would be good; there is cold beer for sale down the street at Ralph's," before acting out the conclusion: walking to Ralph's. But we do commonly devote conscious attention to the formation and testing of hypotheses relevant to the fulfillment of our desires. A beer drinker in a new city devotes conscious attention to the formation and testing of the minor premise, "there is cold beer for sale down the street at Ralph's," and, in general, when one first seeks to fulfill a new desire, or when changing circumstances make it impossible to fulfill an existing desire by habitual means, one consciously entertains and tests hypotheses about what means are conducive to one's ends. This is why condition 2 in the above definition stresses that the practical reasoning in question involves both drawing inferences and hypothesis formation and testing. What separates desire from instinct and simple habit is the special kind of learning involved in hypothesis formation and testing. And the easiest way to show that an animal is incapable of having desires is to show that it is incapable of this kind of learning.

It is also important to remember that people are not continually conscious of the desires on which they are acting. I can desire cold beer all the way to the store without thinking of beer at every step. This is why condition 3 is only that the practical reasoning in question be potentially conscious. The paradigm of desiring behavior is found not when I walk habitually to Ralph's but when, unexpectedly, Ralph's is closed. Only then am I forced to engage in conscious practical reasoning about how to procure cold beer. A habitual trip to Ralph's expresses a desire for cold beer if the habit formed as a result of previous conscious practical reasoning, but it ceases to express the desire if I am no longer capable of conscious practical reasoning.

My third reason for believing that the above definition accurately captures the core concept of desire is that it sheds significant light on our otherwise muddled intuitions about which nonhuman organisms have desires. Somewhere between my cat and a rutabaga, the concept of "desire" becomes inapplicable, but it is difficult to say exactly where. Birds seem to be a slightly more puzzling case than mammals, and, as I move on to herpetofauna (reptiles and amphibians) and to fish and invertebrates, I am increasingly hesitant to say that these animals "really" have desires. However, with the above definition in hand, one can make a careful examination of certain behavioral and physiological comparisons between normal, adult humans (the paradigm case of animals that have desires) and various other organisms to explain one's initial perplexity and to allow one to say with more assurance which animals "really" have desires and why.

BEHAVIORAL COMPARISONS: MULTIPLE REVERSAL AND PROBABILITY LEARNING

Because any number of things, including plants and thermostats, appear to be goal directed, and because consciousness (in the familiar, phenomenological sense) cannot be directly observed, the best place to start is with the special kind of learning that hypothesis formation and testing represents—that is, with condition 2. Condition 1—goal directedness—although very important when the question is, "What particular desires does this entity have?" is not very important when, as now, we are trying to determine which kinds of entities have desires. Condition 3—consciousness—is very important when we turn from considering behavioral evidence to considering physiological evidence. We must then decide what we mean by "conscious" before we can assess the significance of certain physiological evidence.[2] For now, however, I use certain behavioral studies of

---

2. The distinction between behavioral comparisons on the one hand and physiological comparisons on the other is not always clear-cut. For example, when we compare the "flight or fight" response in human and nonhuman animals, we are simultaneously comparing physiological structure and processes (the animals in question have similar nervous, respiratory, and cardiovascular systems) and overt behavior (similar physical movements occur under similar stimulus conditions). Nevertheless, it is useful to separate these two kinds of comparisons and to evaluate them independently, if only because they correspond to two very different manners in which evidence may be gathered. In what follows, by "behavioral comparisons" I mean exclusively comparisons of overt movement, and by "physiological comparisons" I mean exclusively comparisons of bodily structure and processes that are not ostensibly observable.

animal learning to shed light on the question without raising the difficult topic of consciousness. If certain animals can be shown to be incapable of hypothesis formation and testing on simple behavioral grounds, then we can say with great certainty that they are incapable of having desires. And, if others clearly are capable of hypothesis formation and testing, then we will need to pay close attention to them when we turn to the physiological evidence and the difficult question of consciousness.

Where "learning" is construed broadly enough, even headless insects can learn. G. A. Horridge developed a classic preparation described in the following passage from a review of the literature on insect learning:

> Pairs of headless insects [cockroaches and locusts] were suspended over containers of electrified saline solution. For one animal (experimental), the leg which was being trained received electric shocks whenever it fell below a predetermined level. For the other animal (control), the corresponding leg was shocked, but without regard to position of the leg. After 30 to 45 minutes of training in this manner, the two animals were separated; and each was shocked independently whenever its own leg fell below the predetermined level. During this second phase of the experiment, the experimental animals received significantly fewer shocks than the control animals. Since both animals had received the same pattern and intensity of shocks in the initial phase of the experiment, the subsequent difference in their performance was attributed to learning of the contingency between leg position and shock in the experimental animal. It was concluded, therefore, that the vental nerve cord is capable of mediating learning. (Alloway 1972, pp. 51–52)

Others later demonstrated the same effect in isolated legs whose connection to a single isolated ganglion of the ventral nerve cord had been retained. The point is that examples of rudimentary learning can be found in organisms that are not plausibly said to be conscious at all, let alone to be consciously formulating and testing hypotheses.

In the mid-1960s, Martin Bitterman claimed to have identified striking discontinuities in learning abilities among animals at various "levels" on the traditionally recognized phylogenetic "scale," discontinuities that do suggest that some animals and not others are capable of hypothesis formation and testing and that map roughly onto commonsense assumptions about the relative intelligence of animals at different locations on the "scale." Talk of various animals' "levels" on a phylogenetic "scale" is misleading. It is biologically inaccurate insofar as it suggests that evolution has a fixed direction, with all more recently evolved organisms being more complex. On the ruling paradigm in evolutionary biology, species are grouped not as so many steps on an evolutionary ladder of increasing complexity but as so many branches of a tree, the higher (more recent) branches of which are not always more complex than the lower. In what follows, I continue to speak in terms of "higher" and "lower" positions on a phylogenetic "scale," but only for economy of expression. The notion that invertebrates, fishes, reptiles and amphibians, birds, and mammals are arrayed in that order in terms of cognitive sophistication and consciousness is very much a part of our commonsense conception of the world, and my point in this chapter is that a careful look at the behavior and neurophysiology of animals suggests that there is good reason for ordering animals in roughly that way, at least as a presumption or general rule (some possible and actual exceptions are noted later).

In an article titled "The Evolution of Intelligence" (1965), Bitterman argues that "brain structures evolved by higher animals do not serve merely to replicate old functions . . . but to mediate new ones," so that, contrary to what was then commonly assumed, qualitative differences in intelligence emerge at various levels on the phylogenetic scale. Bitterman asserts, for example, that no animal at or below the phylogenetic level of a fish exhibits what he calls "progressive adjustment" in "multiple reversal trials." Bitterman designed simple devices to test the speed with which various animals can adapt to the reversal of learned reward patterns. Fish receive meal worms for pressing their heads against the correct plastic disk immersed in their water, while turtles, pigeons, rats, and monkeys receive analogous rewards for pressing the correct buttons in appropriately modified Skinner boxes. Bitterman found that, while it takes any animal longer to learn the new reward pattern the first time the pattern is reversed, reptiles (by which Bitterman means both reptiles and amphibians, i.e., the herpetofauna, or, as students of zoology commonly put it, "herps"), birds, and mammals exhibit progressively faster adaptations to subsequent reversals. Fish and lower animals do not. This "learning curve," Bitterman argues, represents an emergent level of intelligence for which no correlate exists at or below the level of a fish. Herps, curiously, exhibit the curve only when presented with "spatial" rather than "visual" problems (i.e., with problems in which reward is linked to the location rather than the color or shape of presented objects).

The significance of Bitterman's finding is this. The behavior of an animal that, like a fish, takes as long or longer to learn the reward pattern every time it is reversed is more plausibly explained in terms of operant conditioning than in the more cognitive terms of hypothesis formation and testing. The fish's behavior appears to be the result of the force vectors of habit pushing the animal first one way and then the other. Apparently, after each reversal, the force of habit created by the previous reward pattern has to be overcome by the force of habit being created by the new reward pattern before success is achieved. By contrast, when a mammal's behavior alters immediately in response to a new reward pattern, its behavior appears to have leapfrogged the conditioning created by the previous reward pattern, and this leapfrogging suggests that some kind of hypothesis formation and testing is at work.

In related research reported in the same article, Bitterman discovered two more discontinuities in animals' learning abilities. He found a discontinuity in the ways that fish and herps, on the one hand, and birds and mammals, on the other, deal with "probability learning" situations. In a probability learning situation, each possible response is rewarded a fixed percentage of the time, but the rewarded alternative is varied at random. Bitterman found striking dissimilarities in the strategies employed by various types of animals. Fish exhibit a strategy Bitterman calls "matching" (or "random matching"), meaning that they respond randomly but in percentages matching the frequencies with which each alternative is rewarded. Rats and monkeys, by contrast, typically "maximize," meaning that they respond 100% of the time with the more frequently rewarded alternative. In this study, Bitterman found that birds occupy a curious middle ground between mammals and herps, one analogous to the middle ground that herps occupy between birds and fish in multiple reversal trials. Birds, like herps, match on visual problems but, like mammals, maximize on spatial problems. Bitterman concludes that the new "modes of adjustment" displayed by "higher animals" emerge earlier in spatial than in visual contexts—that is, where location rather than color or shape is salient.

Another striking discontinuity Bitterman found is that only mammals exhibit what he calls "systematic" matching in probability learning situations. By "systematic matching," he means either systematically choosing the alternative rewarded in the preceding trial or systematically avoiding the alternative rewarded in the preceding trial (although this second strategy appears only in primates). While acknowledging that systematic matching is no more successful than random matching and is, in fact, less successful than maximizing (where the reward ratio is 70 to 30, the probability of correct choice is 70% when maximizing but only 58%—$(.7 \times .7) + (.3 \times .3)$—when using systematic matching), Bitterman argues that the emergence of systematic matching in the lower mammals was significant, because human subjects consciously attach significance to systematic matching in similar learning situations:

> Systematic matching is no more successful than random matching . . . and yet we know that human subjects employ systematic matching in trying to find a principle that will enable them to make the correct choice 100 percent of the time. If the use of systematic matching by lower [mammals] is based on some crude, strategic capability, it represents a considerable functional advance over random matching. (1965, p. 98)

Here Bitterman suggests that mammals' capacity for systematic matching "represents a considerable functional advance" over herps' and fishes' random matching, because human subjects exercise that capacity during conscious hypothesis formation and testing, in (as Bitterman puts it) "trying to find a principle that will enable them to make the correct choice 100 percent of the time."

I suggest that, for similar reasons, birds' ability to maximize represents a considerable functional advance over herps' and fishes' slavery to random matching. A normal human subject might employ random matching in one attempt at solving an analogous problem. One might think, "Well, now I'll try this: I'll figure out what percentage of the time each alternative is being rewarded, and then I'll respond randomly, but in equal percentages." But an intelligent subject would abandon this strategy after finding out that it paid off less often than maximizing, and a subject who, like a fish, employed no other strategy at all, from beginning to end, would be suspected of not formulating any hypotheses at all. Such a subject's behavior would be readily explainable in terms of the force vectors of habit created by operant conditioning: a 70 to 30 response ratio simply reflects the conflicting forces of habit produced by a 70 to 30 reward ratio. By contrast, when a bird or mammal begins to maximize, it achieves independence from the habituation induced by the alternative being rewarded 30% of the time, and this independence suggests that some kind of hypothesis formation and testing is at work.

Bitterman's two simple lines of research identify three important properties of animal learning that emerge at different levels on the phylogenetic scale. Each one adds strength to the claim that animals that possess it are capable of having desires, because they are capable of hypothesis formation and testing, while subtracting strength from the claim that animals that do not possess it are capable of having desires (these findings are summarized in table 2.1):

1. progressive adjustment in multiple reversal trials emerges with the herps;
2. maximizing in probability learning situations emerges at the avian level; and
3. systematic matching in probability learning situations emerges at the mammalian level.

A human subject who fails to exhibit progressive adjustment in a multiple reversal trial, or who always matches in probability learning situations, could not plausibly be said to be formulating and testing hypotheses. The lack of both skills in fish thus constitutes clear behavioral evidence against the claim that they have desires. At the other extreme, our fellow mammals' ability to either maximize or engage in systematic matching in probability learning situations, coupled with their exhibition of progressive adjustment in multiple reversal trials, constitutes clear behavioral evidence in favor of the claim that they are capable of hypothesis formation and testing. On purely behavioral grounds, then, a case can be made for denying that fish are capable of having desires. We have not yet shown that our fellow mammals have desires, for we have not yet broached the question of whether or not their hypothesis formation and testing is potentially conscious (condition 3 in the core concept of desire). But, on purely behavioral grounds, we have reason to believe that they are capable of hypothesis formation and testing (condition 2), and we have reason to doubt that fish can have desires, because they seem to be incapable of this.

Table 2.1. Bitterman's findings

Multiple reversal		Probability learning
no progressive adjustment	⎧ *fish* ⎫	matching
progressive adjustment	⎧ *herpetofauna** ⎫ ⎨ *birds*** ⎬ ⎩ *mammals* ⎭	maximizing / systematic matching***

*Herps (reptiles and amphibians) exhibit progressive adjustment on spatial problems (those in which the location of presented objects is salient) but not on visual problems (those in which the shape or color of presented objects is salient).

**Birds maximize on spatial problems but not on visual problems.

***Only primates systematically avoid the previously rewarded alternative. Other mammals' systematic matching consists in selecting the previously rewarded alternative.

Birds and herps occupy an interesting middle ground. Herps always match in probability learning situations, on which score they are no more sophisticated than fish, but herps do exhibit progressive adjustment on spatial problems in multiple reversal trials. Thus only one of the three salient comparisons applies to them. The behavioral evidence for saying that herps are capable of hypothesis formation and testing is thus only minimal. Birds are significantly more sophisticated, but the case for saying that they are capable of desire is still somewhat weaker than that for saying that mammals are. Birds do exhibit progressive adjustment in both kinds of multiple reversal trials, and they do maximize on some probability learning problems. So the evidence that birds are capable of having desires is decidedly stronger than that for saying that herps are capable of having desires, but it is weaker than the evidence for saying that mammals are capable of having desires. This is because mammals maximize on both kinds of probability learning problems, whereas birds maximize only on spatial problems, and mammals are capable of switching from maximizing to systematic matching in probability learning situations, whereas birds are incapable of systematic matching.

Two cautionary notes are in order. First, I do not claim to have surveyed every form of learning that might be deemed a sign of conscious practical reasoning in general or to conscious hypothesis formation and testing in particular. But, as just explained, Bitterman's observations about reversal and probability learning are at least prima facie relevant to the possession of these capacities, and his observations about the ways these capacities emerge as we climb "the phylogenetic scale" map remarkably well onto the commonsense presumptions about the emergence of consciousness and intelligence. Bitterman—and common sense—may ultimately be shown wrong. But I have sought in vain for decisive refutation of the general scenario he describes. For example, for several years I have asked fish scientists whether they thought fish would exhibit progressive adjustment in multiple reversal trials, and, although several felt confident they would, I have found no confirmation of this in the literature.[3] A more likely source of disconfirmation is the invertebrate realm. As Bitterman put it quite recently, "what we know about learning in animals [still] comes primarily from intensive work with a small number of *vertebrate* species . . . and only with [a] few species has it gone much beyond the question of whether they are capable of learning at all" (1988, p. 251, emphasis added).

This brings me to the second cautionary note. I have made several generalizations about very broad taxa: mammals, birds, herps, fish, and all the invertebrates taken together. Such generalizations are dangerous, because much of the research on learning has been conducted on just a few species from each of these taxa. Even if claims about these tested species' abilities are well grounded, this does not of itself ensure that the generalization applies to all species in the class or phylum in question. Convergent evolution of gross physical structures (e.g., raptoral feet in both the owl and hawk families) is a common phenomenon, and, among invertebrates, other brain structures may have evolved to support what we now think of as typically higher-vertebrate learning strategies. A striking example, discussed later in this chapter, is the cephalopods (octopi, squid, and cuttlefish), which have evolved much larger brains and proportionately greater learning capacities than other invertebrates.

Physiological Comparisons: The Mammalian Prefrontal Cortex

On purely behavioral grounds, then, we can say that fish probably are not capable of having desires, because they are not capable of hypothesis formation and testing. On the other hand, mammals clearly are capable, and birds and herps occupy an interesting middle ground. A similar picture emerges in regard to physiological comparisons, but a lengthy argument and a discussion of what it means to be conscious will be necessary to establish this. Here again our guidepost is the normal adult human (the paradigm case of an animal capable of having desires). We begin by asking, "Where is it most plausible to say that desire (or at least the

---

3. The one exception is an article reporting that, while individual members of a species of schooling fish from shallow streams in Venezuela do not exhibit progressive adjustment in multiple reversal trials, small groups of the fish do (Levin and Vergara 1987).

hypothesis formation and testing characteristic of desire) is localized in the human nervous system?"

In asking this question, I assume that the problem of other minds has been solved for our fellow adult human beings. I assume that, as a general rule, when an adult reports that he or she is conscious of certain things and not conscious of others, he or she is correct. I do not assume that all such reports are true or even that we have privileged access to our conscious states. We can lie, and I assume that we are sometimes mistaken about what we are and are not conscious of. But I do assume that, as a general rule, when an otherwise normal adult suffers damage to some part of his central nervous system, his or her reports about what he or she is then conscious of can be used as a measure of the effect of the injury on his or her consciousness.

I also assume that human consciousness supervenes upon certain neurophysiological states of the human nervous system. In assuming this, I do not mean to rule out consciousness in entities that, like complex computers, have no neurons at all but do have nonneuronal networks that function analogously. Whether or not consciousness can be attributed to such entities is discussed in the following section. In assuming that consciousness supervenes upon neurophysiological states, I mean only to emphasize that, if we are confident that certain parts of the human nervous system support certain kinds of consciousness, and if we know that other organisms' nervous systems are relevantly similar to ours, then we can be confident that these other organisms are conscious in ways similar to us.

Under the two assumptions just discussed, the case for saying that a nonhuman animal has desires will be strongest where

(a) the nonhuman animal's nervous system includes that part that, in human beings, is associated with conscious hypothesis formation and testing (conditions 2 and 3 in the core concept of desire) and

(b) the part in question functions analogously as measured in behavioral terms.

In this section, I argue that all and only mammals fall into this category. In the next section, I consider what we are to make of animals that, like birds, lack that part of the central nervous system associated with desire in us but nevertheless seem to have another part that functions analogously.

In reviewing the relevant neurophysiological evidence, one must bear in mind four basic statements of comparative neurophysiology, each of which is a statement about one of four broad categories into which all vertebrates can be grouped: fish, herpetofauna, birds, and mammals (taken here to include marsupials and the platypus). Vertebrate brains, like those of many invertebrates, are divided into three major parts: a hindbrain, a midbrain, and a forebrain. Vertebrates are distinguished from all lower animals by the relative development of the forebrain and, in particular, by the presence of a recognizable cerebrum. However, only in herps does a small amount of cerebral cortex first appear. Fish have no cerebral cortex. Our first two statements regarding comparative neurophysiology, then, are the following:

(S1) fish are distinguished from all lower animals by the presence of a recognizable cerebrum, and

(S2) herps are distinguished from all lower animals by the presence of a cerebral cortex.

The birds and mammals (the higher vertebrates) evolved from the same primitive reptilian stock, and both are distinguished from the lower vertebrates by the relative development of the cerebrum. Different portions of the avian and mammalian cerebra have developed during evolution, however. In birds, the base of the cerebrum, the striatum, is highly developed and the cap of the cerebrum, the cerebral cortex, is vestigial. In mammals, the situation is reversed: the cortex has expanded, overgrowing and covering the striatum, and the most highly developed portion of the avian striatum, the hyperstriatum, is entirely absent. Today, ethologists generally take development of the cerebral cortex to be the best measure of relative intelligence among mammalian species and development of the hyperstriatum to be the best measure of relative intelligence among avian species (Stettner and Matyniak 1980). However, for reasons that will become apparent in what follows, I wish to emphasize that an identifiable prefrontal lobe is found in the cerebral cortex of all mammals but in no bird (Fuster 1989, p. 6). Thus my third and fourth statements regarding comparative neurophysiology are the following:

(S3) the hyperstriatum is the dominant structure in the avian cerebrum and birds are distinguished from all lower animals by the presence of this structure, and

(S4) mammals are distinguished from all lower animals by the presence of a prefrontal cortex.

With these four statements in mind, I begin to assess the relevant physiological evidence. In *Animal Liberation*, Peter Singer gives the following reason for focusing on the diencephalon (a part of the midbrain) when considering physiological evidence for the moral considerability of nonhuman animals:

> Although humans have a more developed cerebral cortex than other animals, this part of the brain is concerned with thinking functions rather than with basic impulses, emotions, and feelings. These impulses, emotions, and feelings are located in the diencephalon, which is well developed in many other species of animals, especially mammals and birds. (1990, p. 11)

Singer is correct to focus on the diencephalon, because he identifies having interests with having the capacity to suffer, and bodily pain is commonly assumed to enter consciousness in the thalamus.[4] However, given the stronger, more narrow analysis of desire upon which we have settled, being susceptible to pain is not sufficient for having desires. The bare consciousness of pain, in and of itself, could at most constitute what Feinberg calls "a brute longing for I know not what."

The diencephalon is, in a very real sense, involved in desire, because most sensory information is initially processed there. Thus damage to the diencephalon impairs an individual's capacity for desire insofar as it impairs the individual's ability to process sensory data and thereby to construct an accurate representation of the world. But such damage will not directly impair the individual's capacity for conscious practical reasoning, and that capacity rather than sentience per se is the sine qua non of desire. In attempting to localize desire, we need to look for a portion of the brain to which damage directly impairs the individual's ability consciously to reason about what to do in light of this representation of the world.

Neurophysiologists recognized early on that the prefrontal lobe is different from other regions of the cerebral cortex. Numerous studies have shown that, while electrical stimulation of any other region produces sensation, bodily movement, or vivid memory recall, stimulation of the prefrontal cortex produces none of these and that damage to the area produces no immediately observable disorders of sensation or movement. On the other hand, it is well known that frontal lobe lesions can produce grave personality disorders. In an early and famous case, a Vermont construction worker named Phinneas Gage lost most of his left frontal lobe when an explosion drove an iron rod a yard long and over an inch in diameter into his cheek and out the top front of his skull. Gage's miraculous physical recovery, which strained the credulity of the mid-nineteenth-century medical community, was marred by what John Harlow, his personal physician, characterized as a release of "animal passions" in a previously "well-balanced mind" (Harlow 1868, p. 340).[5]

4. The reason for this assumption is that damage to the portion of the cerebrum devoted to bodily sensation (the somatosensory cortex) does not destroy awareness of bodily pain. Only the "ability to localize the stimulus or to discriminate its intensity is severely impaired" by injuries of the somatosensory cortex. Conversely, when damage is limited to the thalamus, "thalamic pain"—intense pain triggered by minor bodily contact—results (Nolte 1981, p. 177).

5. Traces of Luria's (1966) characterization of frontal syndrome are evident in Harlow's description of Gage at the time he reapplied for his old job, seven months after the accident: "His contractors, who regarded him as the most efficient and capable foreman in their employ previous to his injury, considered the change in his mind so marked that they could not give him his place again. The equilibrium or balance, so to speak, between his intellectual faculties and animal propensities, seems to have been destroyed. He is fitfull, irreverent, indulging at times in the grossest profanity (which was not previously his custom), manifesting but little deference for his fellows, impatient of restraint or advice when it conflicts with his desires, at times pertinaciously obstinate, yet capricious and

While experience with approximately 40,000 frontal lobotomies performed between 1935 and the early 1960s, and a number of spectacular accidents like Gage's, have popularized the view, prevalent among neurophysiologists prior to the turn of the century, that the prefrontal cortex is the seat of distinctively human personality traits, attempts to characterize "frontal syndrome" more precisely have focused primarily on the cognitive aspects of frontal lobe damage. The classic study is Aleksandr Luria's *Higher Cortical Functions in Man*. Luria's findings clearly suggest that damage to the prefrontal cortex directly and critically affects a human being's ability to meet each of the three conditions of the core concept of desire.

Luria found that "frontal patients" (as he calls patients with major injuries to the prefrontal cortex [Fuster 1989, p. 9]) can perform perfectly well "customary actions [and] well-consolidated manipulations with objects." But on a broad range of tasks requiring action, as Luria puts it, "in accordance with a preformed plan," frontal patients' behavior is disrupted by irrelevant stimuli that would be ignored by normal individuals. In place of discriminating behavior that efficiently achieves the goal in question, frontal patients perseverate or exhibit "irrelevant stereotyped reactions." Striking examples are scattered through Luria's book. He describes a patient who, while being asked to write certain words down on paper, began writing down elements of conversations he overheard around him; another patient, a carpenter, planed a piece of wood until nothing was left of it and then went right on planing the bench. Such patients' behavior, Luria writes, "was determined not by specialized, selective systems of connections, but by irrelevant stimuli, which [were] perceived without any kind of discrimination and which quickly evoked a motor reaction" (1966, pp. 294, 306).

A typical frontal patient has no trouble squeezing a hollow bulb in the hand on command but has great trouble learning to squeeze in response to a red light but not in response to a green light, an instruction that reverses the patient's habitual response patterns. Luria writes:

> this generalized informative meaning of stimuli, formulated in a general rule, is extremely difficult, and sometimes impossible, to produce in patients with massive lesions of the frontal lobes. Even if the necessary conditioned reflex can in fact be formed . . . these patients cannot formulate the appropriate rule. When

---

vacillating, devising many plans of future operation, which are no sooner arranged than they are abandoned in turn for others appearing more feasible. A child in his intellectual capacity and manifestations, he has the animal passions of a strong man. Previous to his injury, though untrained in the schools, he possessed a well-balanced mind, and was looked upon by those who knew him as a shrewd, smart business man, very energetic and persistent in executing all his plans of operation. In this regard his mind was radically changed, so decidedly that his friends and acquaintances said he was 'no longer Gage' " (Harlow 1868, pp. 339–40).

questioned, they cannot say why they gave a motor response to one signal but refrained from doing so at the appearance of the other signal. Frequently they are not even aware that they gave a motor response to the signal when it appeared, and when asked why they pressed, they answer: "Because you told me to." (p. 313)

All of this suggests that frontal patients have difficulty pursuing a goal (condition 1 in the core concept of desire), even in accordance with a ready-made plan, if doing so requires conscious attention to the plan rather than raw habituation (condition 3).

Luria also noted that, while normal individuals quickly develop efficient strategies for discovering while blindfolded which letter is being presented to them on a board of raised blocks, the performance of frontal patients on this problem does not steadily improve, suggesting that frontal patients have difficulty formulating their own hypotheses (condition 2):

Tests have shown that normal subjects, after touching such structures, at first make many searching movements, but later they conduct their search in a manner adequate to the program, reduce their movements, and begin to pick out the heuristic points selectively, and so quickly reach the necessary solution.

The process of finding the necessary programs is totally different in character in patients with a marked frontal syndrome. . . . [Such patients] start to solve this problem by touching the letters presented to them, but their search is chaotic in character and their searching movements are not guided by definite hypotheses. These patients do not begin to pick out elements carrying the greatest information and providing evidence of the most likely solution to the problem. (p. 325)

Although damage to other lobes of the cerebrum can produce ostensibly similar motor deficits, damage to the prefrontal lobe is unique insofar as frontal patients fail to recognize errors in performance, and, even when told of their errors, they typically do not make a conscious attempt to correct them. This suggests that frontal patients also have difficulty testing hypotheses (condition 2, again). A patient with a lesion of the motor cortex or of the portion of the parietal lobe concerned with drawing may have ostensibly similar difficulties controlling his or her drawing movements but will recognize mistakes and will make a conscious effort to correct them. A frontal patient, by contrast, typically will be unaware of making mistakes and, when mistakes are pointed out, will be unable to correct them, despite the fact that his or her parietal lobe and motor cortex are undamaged.

In the mid-1960s, advances in techniques used to measure electrical activity in the brain allowed researchers to observe a phenomenon that tends to confirm Luria's view that the prefrontal cortex is involved in conscious attention to a problem or plan. Researchers repeatedly presented human subjects with an audible click followed by a series of flashes. During the initial presentations, a wave-shaped variation in the amplitude of brain waves in the prefrontal cortex occurred in response to each. However, when subjects were instructed to terminate the series of flashes by pressing a button, very different results were obtained: a large negative variation began with the click and ended only when the flashes were extinguished by the button press. This change in amplitude came to be called the "contingent negative variation" (or CNV), because its occurrence was shown to be contingent upon the degree of association between the click and the flashes. To the degree that the association was weakened by including clicks that were not followed by the flashes, the CNV was proportionately attenuated. A strong negative variation still accompanied the onset of the flashes, however, suggesting that negative variation in amplitude is a sign of conscious attention to salient cues (Walter et al. 1964; Tecce and Scheff 1969). Thus damage to the prefrontal cortex adversely affects a human being's ability to muster conscious attention to problem solving (condition 3, again).

The evidence reviewed so far suggests that in human beings at least, the capacity for conscious practical reasoning is localized in the prefrontal cortex. This is not to say that all one has to have in order to have desires is an intact prefrontal cortex. Desire, like other complex cognitive phenomena, probably cannot in that sense be localized in any particular portion of the central nervous system. The prefrontal cortex is an associational area, and other (e.g., perceptual) areas must be functioning if an associational area is to have something to associate. Nor should I be understood to say that, if the prefrontal cortex is damaged or removed, one will straightway cease to do the things one previously desired to do. After a prefrontal lobotomy, I would doubtless still go to the store and buy cold beer, since this is an habitual behavior involving (in Luria's phrase) "well-consolidated manipulations of objects," and successful performance of it does not require conscious hypothesis formation and testing. But if after the lobotomy I were unable to adjust to unusual conditions (e.g., Ralph's being closed), then my going to the store would no longer be a manifestation of a desire for cold beer.

Our fellow mammals' possession of a prefrontal cortex is strong prima facie evidence for their having desires as well. However, ostensibly similar structures sometimes function very differently in the brains of different species of animals. For instance, the ostensibly similar pineal glands of fish, amphibians, and many reptiles have photoreceptor cells that apparently help trigger seasonal cycles, but there is no functional analog to these cells in the human pineal gland. However, the prefrontal cortexes in human and nonhuman mammals are remarkably similar in architecture, and experiments with nonhuman animals have produced behavioral results directly analogous to those just discussed. The CNV phenomenon has been observed in monkeys (Fuster 1989, p. 93). Also, monkeys, dogs, cats, and rats whose prefrontal cortex has been damaged or removed ("frontal animals") are deficient in ways that directly parallel the clinical phenomena Luria observed. Luria found that frontal patients have difficulty performing actions "in accordance with a preformed plan," because they are so easily distracted by irrelevant stimuli. Similarly, animal researchers find that, if there is an enforced delay between stimulus and response, a frontal animal has unusual difficulty learning the correct response, and they attribute the deficit to the animal's "fundamental difficulty in suppressing its attention to irrelevant stimuli" (Fuster 1989, p. 82). Just as Luria found that frontal patients fail to adjust subsequent behavior in light of past errors, researchers find that frontal animals are "unable to benefit from errors," and, just as Luria's frontal patients have trouble inverting habitual response patterns, frontal animals lose the progressive adjustment in multiple reversal trials characteristic of normal mammals, a deficit researchers attribute to the animals' being "unable to . . . adjust to [a] change in the rules of the game" (Fuster 1989, p. 53).

When we discuss the scope of nonmetaphorical desire in the animal kingdom, the most significant physiological comparison we can make between a normal human and any nonhuman animal is to show that it has a prefrontal cortex that functions analogously to the way the lobe functions in the human being. In this section, I have shown that this most salient comparison applies to all and only our fellow mammals. Thus there is a parallel between the behavioral evidence considered in the previous section and the physiological evidence I am here surveying: in each case, the strongest comparison that can be made between human and nonhuman animals applies to all and only our fellow mammals. When, in the next section, I confront the difficult question of consciousness head on, I show why the physiological evidence fully parallels the behavioral evidence.

PHYSIOLOGICAL COMPARISONS: THE AVIAN HYPERSTRIATUM
AND THE REPTILIAN CEREBRUM

Without worrying much about the concept of consciousness, the behavioral and the physiological evidence considered thus far together suggest that normal mammals have desires while animals at and "below" the phylogenetic level of fish do not. However, when we turn to the taxa in between, to birds and to herpetofauna, we cannot avoid addressing the concept of consciousness directly.

The difficulty can best be framed in terms of the controversy over functionalism versus the identity theory in the philosophy of mind. Functionalists identify being in a particular type of psychological state with being in a particular type of brain state. This is, initially, a very plausible position. It seems reasonable, for example, to identify being in pain with having certain neurons excited, presumably whichever ones are associated with the consciousness of pain.

A problem with this view is that it would require us to constrict implausibly the scope of various psychological phenomena. To see why this is so, consider the foregoing example of being in pain. How are we to decide which neurons must be excited for one to be in a state of pain? If we base it on our own experiences with human brains, or even on what we suppose are the experiences of our fellow mammals, then we may be forced to say that many animals that otherwise appear to be in pain really are not. For example, if we identified being in a state of pain with having certain neurons excited in the cerebral cortex,[6] then no animal that, like a bird, lacks a cerebral cortex could be said to be in pain. Similarly, if we identify "believing that 2 + 2 = 4" with having certain neurons excited in the cerebral cortex, then an android like Star Trek's Commander Data, who has no brain cells at all, but only silicon circuits, could never be said to believe that 2 + 2 = 4. In such cases, behavioral evidence seems to force us to abandon the proposed identifications. We believe that the bird is in pain, because it exhibits the fight or flight response (its heart rate goes up, its pupils constrict, adrenalin is secreted, etc.) and because it flails about and screeches. We are convinced that Data believes that 2 + 2 = 4, because he responds correctly in a variety of ways—for example, he correctly infers that there are four apples in the room from the facts that there are two on the table and two in the refrigerator.

Such objections to the identity theory have led to its rejection in most quarters. Functionalism is now the most widely endorsed theory among philosophers of mind. Functionalists identify a particular type of psychological state in terms of its functional interrelationships with other psychological states and the behavioral outputs these relationships produce under varying environmental conditions. A functionalist would have no problem saying that a bird is in pain when it behaves in the foregoing ways, even if birds lacked entirely the particular brain cells that fire when we are in pain. And a functionalist would have no problem saying that Data believes that 2 + 2 = 4 just as we do. For a functionalist, having a mind does not imply having any particular sort of hardware. If the existence of certain interrelated mental states provides the most parsimonious explanation of our own behavior under analogous conditions, then we have good reason to attribute analogous mental processess to the bird and to Data, however different is the hardware running the processes.

The significance of this controversy for our topic is this. All and only mammals have a prefrontal lobe in their brains, and among mammals the capacity for conscious practical reasoning seems to be localized there. If we adopted a version of the identity theory and identified having desires with having a certain pattern of neuronal activity in the prefrontal cortex, then we could say confidently that all and only mammals have desires. However, to do so we would have to ignore

---

6. I suggest this purely for the sake of constructing a dramatic example. It would be grossly implausible to identify being in a state of pain with having certain cortical neurons excited, for the reasons given above in the text: pain enters human consciousness below the cortical level.

as irrelevant much of the behavioral evidence surveyed above. In particular, we would have to dismiss as irrelevant the facts that both normal human beings and birds maximize in probability learning situations and that both normal human beings and herps exhibit progressive adjustment on multiple reversal trials. We would have to claim that, of the three behavioral comparisons considered, only the capacity for systematic matching (which alone is uniquely mammalian) constitutes a relevant comparison. But this would be no more plausible than dismissing as irrelevant the behavior that leads us to say that Data believes that $2 + 2 = 4$ or that a bird is in pain.

If, on the other hand, we embrace a functionalist account of desires, then the physiological evidence for the presence of desires will directly parallel the behavioral: on both scores, mammals almost certainly have desires, fish almost certainly do not, and birds and herps occupy an ambiguous middle ground. This is because the question of which brain structures are sufficiently functionally analogous to the mammalian prefrontal cortex will ultimately have to be decided on behavioral grounds, and it turns out that birds and herps lose the behavioral features discussed above when they sustain damage to the distinctive brain structures mentioned earlier (in statements S_3 and S_2, respectively).

Damage to the avian hyperstriatum produces severe performance deficits and in particular destroys birds' ability for progressive adjustment in multiple reversal trials, whereas extensive damage to the avian cortex produces no significant effects (Stettner and Matyniak 1980, pp. 198–99). This suggests that in birds the ability to engage in hypothesis formation and testing is localized in the hyperstriatum rather than in the cerebral cortex, as in mammals. The only remaining question is whether or not this processing is potentially conscious. On a functionalist account of desire, however, we already have good evidence that birds engage in conscious practical reasoning of the relevant kind, precisely because they do behave in relevantly similar ways in relevantly similar circumstances. Although they never exhibit systematic matching, birds do maximize in probability learning situations (at least on spatial problems), and they do exhibit progressive adjustment in multiple reversal trials.

The situation is similar with respect to herps, except that the case for saying that they have desires is decisively weaker than that for saying that birds do. Of the three salient behavioral comparisons considered, herps meet only one: they exhibit progressive adjustment in multiple reversal trials, and this only on spatial problems.

So if we embrace a functionalist account of desire, then the physiological evidence precisely parallels the behavioral evidence. (See table 2.2.) Fish and lower animals probably do not have desires. Mammals almost certainly have desires, and in them the practical reasoning characteristic of desire is localized in the prefrontal cortex. Birds probably have desires (although the case for saying that they do is somewhat weaker than that for saying that mammals do), and in

Table 2.2. Parallels between the behavioral and physiological comparisons considered in chapter 2

Behavior		Physiology
none	*Fish*	none
progressive adjustment in multiple reversal trials first emerges	*Reptiles*	this capacity is localized in the cerebral cortex, which is first present here
maximizing in probability learning situations first emerges	*Birds*	this and the previous capacity are localized in the hyperstriatum, which is present only here
systematic matching in probability learning situations first emerges	*Mammals*	this and the previous capacities are localized in the prefrontal cortex, which is present only here

birds practical reasoning is localized in the hyperstriatum. Herps may have desires (although the case for saying that they do is decisively weaker than that for saying that birds do), and, if herps have desires, the related practical reasoning is localized somewhere in the primitive reptilian cerebrum.[7]

Why, then, would a philosopher be tempted to deny functionalism and deny that any nonmammalian animal has desires? I consider only one argument to this conclusion. It is an argument I once was tempted to embrace under the influence of Thomas Nagel's widely cited 1974 paper, "What Is It Like to Be a Bat?"[8]

Nagel argues that any attempt to reduce mental states to physical states (and a fortiori the kind of reduction attempted by functionalists) will fail to capture the essential subjectivity of consciousness. If an organism is conscious, then "there is something it is like to *be* that organism" (p. 436)—that is, it has a distinctive first-person perspective. The third-person perspective adopted in giving a functionalist reduction must of necessity fail to capture this first-person

7. Bitterman did not do lesion studies to determine where in the reptilian cerebrum the ability for progressive adjustment is localized. But, given that, in both mammals and birds, the ability is localized somewhere in the cerebrum (rather than in, say, the midbrain), it is reasonable to assume that the ability for progressive adjustment is localized somewhere in the cerebrum of the reptiles, from whom both the birds and the mammals evolved.

8. This argument is implicit in the version of this chapter I read to the Illinois Philosophical Association in November 1987 and explicit in the version I read at Washington University in St. Louis during October 1988.

perspective (p. 437). Nagel avoids solipsism by maintaining that "we may ascribe general *types* of experience on the basis of [an] animal's structure and behavior" (p. 439), so that

> There is a sense in which phenomenological facts are perfectly objective: one person can know or say of another what the quality of the other's experience is. They are subjective, however, in the sense that even this objective description of experience is possible only for someone sufficiently similar to the object of ascription to be able to adopt his point of view. (p. 422)

Nagel's reasoning can be applied to functionalist analyses of desire in the following way. Each of us knows what it is like to be an organism with a mammalian prefrontal cortex. Therefore, each of us is "sufficiently similar" to any normal adult mammal to be able to know at least roughly what it is like to be that mammal in the relevant respects.[9] We can adopt the point of view of a nonhuman (but mammalian) animal engaging in any kind of behavior we recognize as similar to behavior we engage in when in pursuit of a desire. However, since the hyperstriatum is entirely absent from our mammalian brains, and since the undifferentiated reptilian cerebral cortex lacks a prefrontal lobe, we can never adopt the perspective of a bird, reptile, or amphibian while it is engaged in behavior we would recognize as the pursuit of a desire in a fellow mammal. Thus, although we can imagine what it is like to be a cat trying to get a toy out from behind the stove, we can never know what it is like to be a bird trying to get a worm out of the ground. In fact, we can never know that there is such a perspective to be adopted. Thus, although nonmammalian vertebrates exhibit overt behavioral patterns that are relevantly similar to those we exhibit in the pursuit of our desires, because we cannot say that there is something it is like to be those nonmammalian vertebrates while performing those behavioral patterns, we can never say that *conscious* practical reasoning is involved. And, therefore, we can never say that any nonmammalian animal has desires—a nonmammalian animal will always fail condition 3 in the core concept of desire.

I now believe that this kind of argument is bound to fail, because it presupposes a solution to the problem of other minds, and the problem of other minds simply cannot be solved without adverting to a functionalist account of consciousness. Neurophysiologists have now shown the intricate interconnections of neurons in the human brain in such detail that no one anymore believes that any particular type of psychological state depends upon the firing of any particular neurons. As researchers are fond of saying, there is no such thing as a "Granny cell" that fires when and only when one sees Granny. Recent developments in parallel distributed processing (PDP) strongly suggest that learning

---

9. Bats, of course, are mammals. Nagel doubts that we can adopt a bat's perceptual perspective, not that we can adopt its reasoning or its problem-solving perspective.

probably occurs as a result of continuous adjustments in connection "weights" among a very large number of simple but highly interconnected neurons (see, e.g., Fodor and Pylyshyn 1988; Bechtel and Abrahamsen 1991). Thus, even among human beings, psychological states are going to have to be typed functionally, in terms of some kind of general pattern of neuronal activity rather than in terms of the firing of particular neurons. To stipulate that the pattern in question must be instantiated in a human or a mammalian brain, or that the neural connections in question must be among neurons in particular lobes of a human or a mammalian cerebrum, would be indefensibly ad hoc. It therefore comes as no surprise to find Thomas Nagel—who wishes to reject functionalist analyses of mental states—using a functionalist criterion for typing mental states in an effort to avoid solipsism. He says that "we may ascribe general *types* of experience on the basis of [an] animal's structure and behavior" (1974, p. 439).

I conclude that the only alternative to the view that some nonmammalian animals have desires is a kind of solipsism—that is, that any given individual can know only that he himself "really" has desires. To avoid this form of solipsism, one must embrace functionalism in the philosophy of mind; but in doing so one must also admit that many nonhuman and some nonmammalian animals "really" have desires.

A CAUTIONARY NOTE ABOUT GENERALIZATIONS

Above, I ended the section on Bitterman's work on learning strategies with a cautionary note. These cautions bear elaboration here in light of the foregoing discussion of physiology and consciousness.

I do not say that the capacity for either or both type(s) of learning discussed above (progressive adjustment on multiple reversal trials and strategies other than matching on probability problems) is a necessary or even a sufficient condition for possessing desires. The argument is an argument by analogy, and arguments by analogy are always more or less strong rather than sound or unsound simpliciter. (As the terms are standardly employed in deductive logic, all arguments by analogy are both invalid and [therefore] unsound.) If a type of organism unambiguously displays both types of learning and has a sophisticated central nervous system, then the case for saying it has desires is very strong. If, on the other hand, an organism neither displays these types of learning nor has a sophisticated central nervous system, then the case for saying it has desires is very weak. Where an organism does not exhibit these two types of learning (or at least we lack evidence that they exhibit them) but the organism does possess a sophisticated central nervous system, then it is important to look for other kinds of learning that seem relevant to the possession of desires. Where this search reveals striking evidence in the affirmative, the case for saying the organism is capable of desire is relatively strong despite lack of evidence for progressive adjustment in multiple reversal trials or for any strategy save matching on probability learning problems. This is the case with octopi.

Although the phylum mollusca includes such simple creatures as bivalves (oysters, clams, scallops, etc.), snails, and slugs, it also includes the cephalopods (octopi, squid, and cuttlefish), which have the most complicated nervous systems of all invertebrates. The intelligence of octopi, in particular, has impressed those who have studied them.

In his classic study, M. J. Wells speculates about why the octopi, which are born precocious and have no dependent childhood and almost no social life, develop such intelligence. First, he notes, they are born only two to three millimeters in length and yet they grow to have an armspan of a meter or more and several kilograms in weight. Consequently, they must continually relearn what is a predator and what is prey. Fish eat them when they are small, but they eat fish at maturity. Plankton, on which they rely when very small, are of little use to them when they are grown. Relatedly, as they grow, soft-bodied octopi must use successively larger cavities for shelter (they generally hunt by night, hiding in crevases during the day), and this means that they must continually relearn their surroundings as they relocate from time to time. Finally, octopi are fast-moving creatures. In addition to crawling with their legs, octopi can propel themselves very suddenly and swiftly using movable "jets" located below their eyes, and they generally seize their prey by springing upon them this way (Wells 1978, pp. 178–79).

The ratio of brain weight to body weight in cephalopods is greater than that of most fish and herps but less than that of most birds and mammals. Moreover, the peripheral nervous systems of cephalopods are extremely well developed (for moving their numerous, highly flexible legs with hundreds of suction cups). In octopi, for instance, the brain constitutes "only the more specialized sensory integrative, higher movement control and learning parts of a rather diffuse nervous system"; an octopus's eight suction-cupped legs contain gangliated cords with almost three times the neurons of the central nervous system (Wells 1978, p. 7). With such large and sophisticated nervous systems, cephalopods in general, and octopi in particular, are prime candidates for an exception to the generalization advanced earlier in this chapter based on Bitterman's survey of learning strategies, namely that no invertebrates have desires.

There is only limited evidence of a learning curve in reversal trials with octopi (Wells 1978, pp. 208–9), and I have been unable to find any studies of probability learning. So, although octopi can easily be trained to distinguish a wide variety of objects and to run mazes, they do not clearly display either of the types of learning on which Bitterman focused. If octopi unambiguously exhibited both types of learning, then, in light of their central nervous system development, I would say that very probably they are capable of desire. But, without unequivocal evidence of these two types of learning, I am more hesitant. Their central nervous system development makes them prime candidates, but, without unambiguous evidence of these two types of learning, I hesitate to conclude that they have desires.

This is a case where a search for other learning abilities is called for. Octopi have greatly impressed experimenters, and some of the learning they have been shown to be capable of does suggest that they have desires. One of the most remarkable relevant examples is a recent study of observational learning. Octopi were trained to discriminate between different colored balls, specifically to attack one to receive a food reward (a piece of fish attached to the far side of the ball, out of sight of the octopus) and to leave the other alone to avoid an electric shock. These trained octopi were then placed in chambers adjacent to untrained octopi and given four more trials with the balls while the untrained individuals watched. Subsequently, the observing octopi were presented with both balls. Those who had observed trained octopi tended, to a very significant degree (P < 0.01), to attack the ball the trained octopi had learned to attack (Fiorito and Scotto 1992, p. 545). Observational learning, like the two types of learning focused on in this chapter, suggests hypothesis formation and testing (although, I would argue, it is not as elemental as they are). As the authors of this study put it, "Copying of a model . . . has been considered preliminary to conceptual thought; in this sense it appears related to the cognitive abilities of the animal learning system." Observational learning has been found in various vertebrates but never before in invertebrates (p. 546).

Experimenters who work with octopi repeatedly remark on how individualized their behavior is capable of becoming, how seemingly intelligent they are, and therefore how easy it is to identify with them. Wells puts it this way:

> It is very easy to identify with *Octopus vulgaris*, even with individuals, because they respond in a very "human" way. They watch you. They come to be fed and they will run away with every appearance of fear if you are beastly to them. Individuals develop individual and sometimes very irritating habits, squirting water or climbing out of their tanks when you approach—and it is all too easy to come to treat the animal as a sort of aquatic dog or cat.
>   Therein lies the danger. (1978, p. 8)

Wells goes on to caution that anthropomorphizing a mollusk is more likely to lead one astray than anthropomorphizing a fellow mammal, because the cephalopods, while very sophisticated in neurological and behavioral characteristics, are very different on both scores from mammals.

Later in the book, Wells describes a neurological difference that causes behavior dramatically different from that of mammals. Apparently, the proprioceptive information provided by the extensive peripheral nervous system of octopi is unavailable to their central nervous systems, and this causes octopi to perform less well than would be expected on some problems (1978, p. 236).

Proprioceptive information is internally generated information about the orientation of the animal's legs. In octopi, the information is used locally within the arms to adjust tensions, but it appears to be unavailable to their brains for problem solving. This would explain why octopi perform poorly on problems involving manipulation of objects, problems that are simple for rats or cats with ostensibly less versatile limbs (p. 243). Also, this would explain why octopi can no longer distinguish shapes, weights, or sizes of objects after being blinded (p. 217), and those whose statocysts have been removed have grave difficulty running simple mazes (statocysts are the cephalopods' mechanism for orienting their visual fields with respect to gravity) (pp. 237–39). An octopus's suction-cupped arms are capable of amazing things, but octopi appear not to be fully aware of how they do things with their arms.

Wells concludes:

> Simply because it is evidently intelligent and possessed of eyes that look back at us, we should not fall into the trap of supposing that we can interpret its behavior in terms of concepts derived from birds or mammals. This animal lives in a very different world from our own. . . . The octopus is an alien. (1978, pp. 9, 8)

Still, I would say that octopus's striking abilities give us reason to think they probably have desires. They at least occupy an ambiguous middle ground between the higher vertebrates and the lower vertebrates, and this illustrates my point in this section: generalizations about broad taxa based on studies of a few species are tentative and subject to exceptions.

PAIN WITHOUT DESIRES?

The evidence presented in this chapter gives us good reason to believe that at least all mammals and birds are capable of having desires, and, although the evidence is weaker than that for saying that birds have desires, there is also reason to believe that reptiles, amphibians, and cephalopods are capable of desire. Significantly, this raises the question of whether or not it is possible to feel pain without desiring to end it, because the consensus view (at least among those who do not dismiss as anthropomorphic all attributions of consciousness to animals) is that all vertebrates, not just mammals, birds, and herps, are capable of feeling pain.

Less research is available to help answer the question, "Which animals can feel pain?" than is available to help answer the question, "Which animals can learn?" This is because the concept of learning can easily be operationalized without reference to consciousness, whereas the concept of being in pain cannot: "pain" is distinguished from "nociception" precisely on this score. Nociceptors are neural end-organs specializing in the detection of damaging or potentially damaging stimuli, and "nociception" means the registering of information in the nervous system about tissue damage or the imminence of tissue damage. Non-human mammals and birds have the same two types of nociceptors in their peripheral nervous systems as humans. In humans, one type of nociceptor is associated with "rapid pain," acute but transient pain leading to rapid withdrawal from a noxious stimulus, and a different one with "slow pain" in damaged tissues, the type of pain that inhibits rather than encourages movement. But a nociceptor firing in the peripheral nervous system (in a finger, say) does not produce pain until that signal is received and interpreted by the brain in certain ways. A standard but compelling way of illustrating this is to note that emotional and cognitive states of the central nervous system are known to inhibit radically the perception of pain. For example, athletes and soldiers commonly report no memory of being in pain after doing something that would have been very painful in a state of less intense concentration or in a less emotionally charged state. So it is quite natural to think of pain as "conscious nociception," and, that being the case, many researchers who have been socialized to fear anthropomorphizing animals have avoided talking about pain in animals (see, generally, Rollin 1989).

To be sure, a good deal of research has been done on pain using mammals (especially rats, cats, pigs, and monkeys) and some on birds, but little systematic research has been done trying to isolate functional nociceptors in lower vertebrates and invertebrates (Rose and Adams 1989, p. 49; Smith and Boyd 1991, p. 63). This is not surprising, perhaps, given that the U.S. Animal Welfare Act excludes from its purview all cold-blooded animals (i.e., everything except mammals and birds). Nevertheless, the authors of the most detailed treatments of the issue to date—by Margaret Rose and David Adams (1989), David DeGrazia and Andrew Rowan (1991), Patrick Bateson (1991), and a working party convened by Britain's Institute of Medical Ethics (consisting of eighteen scientists, medical researchers, and philosophers, including R. G. Frey [Smith and Boyd 1991])—have all reached the same conclusion: while all vertebrates probably can feel pain, most invertebrates probably cannot (the notable exception being the cephalopods).

Like the comparative argument about the mental states of nonhuman animals, the comparative argument in defense of the claim that animals from various species are capable of feeling pain is an argument by analogy. Table 2.3 summarizes six comparisons that were made in most or all of the aforementioned studies. As the table shows, functional analogs of mammalian nociceptors have yet to be found in fish and herps (comparison 1), but endogenous opiods (or opiatelike substances) have been found in all vertebrates and in a variety of invertebrates, including insects, planaria, and earthworms (comparison 4; Rollin 1981, pp. 31–32; Rose and Adams 1989, pp. 55, 61; Smith and Boyd 1991, p. 63). These considerations, taken in isolation, suggest either that no cold-blooded animals feel pain (placing the stress on comparison 1) or that all animals feel pain (putting the stress on comparison 4). When the comparisons are taken as a

Table 2.3. Comparisons relevant to consciousness of pain in the animal kingdom

	Invertebrates			Vertebrates			
	Earth-worms	Insects	Cephalopods	Fish	Herps[a]	Birds	Mammals
1. Nociceptors present	?	–	?[b]	–[c]	–[c]	+	+
2. Central nervous system	–	–	+[d]	+	+	+	+
3. Nociceptors connected to central nervous system	–	–	?/+[e]	?/+[f]	?/+[f]	?/+[f]	+
4. Endogenous opiods present	+	+	?	+	+	+	+
5. Responses modified by analgesics	?	?	?	?	?	+	+
6. Response to damaging stimuli analogous to humans'[g]	–	–	+[h]	+	+	+	+

Source: Adapted, with indicated modifications and qualifications, from Smith and Boyd (1991, p. 63).

Note: A + indicates a positive comparison between the animals in question and normal humans; a – indicates a negative comparison; and a ? indicates inadequate data for making the comparison.

[a]Reptiles and amphibians have been collapsed into a single category. Smith and Boyd score both taxa identically.

[b]Notice, however, Rose and Adams' (1989) conclusion cited in note c, below. With regard to cephalopods, they argue that responses to electric shock are evidence of nociception (p. 48). As noted above in the text, however, even decapitated cockroaches can be habituated to avoid shocks. The more salient reason for expecting to find nociceptors in cephalopods is the overall similarity of their behavior to humans' in situations that would cause us pain (note h, below).

[c]Rose and Adams do conclude that "Evidence supports the existence of nociception in all vertebrates" (p. 49), but this is on the basis of avoidance behavior rather than identification of functioning nociceptors. Smith and Boyd's – implies that here, unlike in the case of earthworms and cephalopods, a disciplined (but still unsuccessful) search for nociceptors has been conducted.

[d]Changed from ? to + in light of Wells (1978) and Young (1965).

[e]Changed from ? to ?/+ in light of the fact that both Young's and Wells's "models of learning in octopi include a 'pain' pathway leading to the vertical lobe of the brain," cited in Smith and Boyd (p. 64).

[f]Changed from ? to ?/+ in light of Rose and Adams's discussion of spinothalamic connections, (pp. 50–51), concluding that "All vertebrates possess neural connections between peripheral nociceptors and central nervous structures."

[g]This category collapses two of Smith and Boyd's: (6) "The animal's response to stimuli that would be painful for a human is functionally similar to the human response (that is, the animal responds so as to avoid or minimize damage to its body)"; and (7) "The animal's behavioral response persists and it shows an unwillingness to resubmit to a painful procedure; [and] the animal can learn to associate apparently nonpainful with apparently painful events" (p. 62). Smith and Boyd give fish and herps a ? on category 6 and a + on category 7.

[h]Changed from ? to + in light of Smith and Boyd's own discussion of the response of octopi to pain (pp. 64–65), that octopi have "distinct and easy-to-recognize responses to noxious stimuli."

package, however, the evidence for saying that invertebrates (with the exception of cephalopods) can feel pain is distinctively weaker than that for saying that vertebrates (including, n.b., fish) can feel pain. Because the consciousness of pain is presumed to require a central nervous system (comparison 2), it is implausible to say that lower invertebrates such as insects, whose nervous systems consist of several loosely organized ganglia, are conscious of pain. This lack of high-level nervous system integration is reflected in insect behaviors that would be very surprising if found in conscious organisms (comparison 6). Insects do not favor damaged limbs or become less active after internal injuries, for instance, and will even sometimes continue to feed normally while being themselves consumed by predators (Smith and Boyd 1991, citing Eisemann et al. 1984). Thus comparison 4, the possession of opiodlike receptors, is the only one suggesting that invertebrates do feel pain. These considerations led the working party of the British Institute of Medical Ethics to conclude, "Much remains to be discovered, but taking the evidence as a whole, the most obvious divide is between the vertebrates and the invertebrates" (Smith and Boyd 1991, p. 64).

This consensus statement may be false; it may be that some of the lower vertebrates are not conscious of pain. On the other hand, my predictions about the scope of desire in the animal kingdom may be false; it may be that all vertebrates are capable of desire. But if I am right that fish probably have no desires and yet feel pain, then apparently it is possible to feel pain without being capable of desiring an end to it. This is an initially strange-sounding conclusion, but I am not squeamish about embracing it, for two reasons.

First, patients commonly report feeling pain but no longer minding it after frontal lobe damage. Second, whatever the scope of desire in the animal kingdom turns out to be, I doubt that it is going to include newborn humans, and yet I am convinced that they feel pain. Neonates' prefrontal cortex is not yet mature. Myelination is the process by which axons become coated with a fatty substance called myelin. This myelin coating improves the efficiency and specificity of message transfer. Although there is controversy on this point, many neurophysiologists take myelination to be a sign of functional maturity (Fuster 1989, pp. 26–29), so that, on the analysis presented here, the late myelination of the human prefrontal cortex may mean that neonatal humans have no desires. Myelination of the human prefrontal cortex does not even begin until two or three months after birth and continues for over ten years. By contrast, the cerebrum of the Rhesus monkey is fully myelinated by the third or fourth postnatal month (Yakovlev and Lecours 1967, p. 5, graph 25, pp. 61, and 69). So, although neonatal humans almost undoubtedly feel pain, if the analysis presented here is accurate, they very well may be incapable of desiring an end to it. Whether a creature that is incapable of having desires nevertheless has interests, and therefore some direct moral standing, is the question to which I turn in the following chapter.

CHAPTER THREE

Biological Interests

Questioning the Mental State Theory of Welfare

M ANY ETHICISTS assume that having desires is not only a sufficient but also a necessary condition for having interests. This is implicit in William James's statement that the "only possible reason there can be why any phenomenon ought to exist is that such a phenomenon actually is desired" (1948, p. 73). In saying this, James commits himself to the belief that an entity that, like a plant,[1] lacks desires can never be of direct moral significance. It can never count for anything in itself but can at most be of instrumental value insofar as its existence satisfies the desires of other beings. Feinberg explicitly argues that

> an interest, however the concept is finally to be analyzed, presupposes at least rudimentary cognitive equipment. Interests are compounded out of *desires* and *aims*, both of which presuppose something like *belief*, or cognitive awareness. (1974, p. 52)

So, he concludes, "mindless creatures have no interests of their own" (p. 53).

Why think otherwise? Tom Regan once responded to Feinberg by arguing that if we pay attention to the distinction between having an interest in something and taking an interest in it (or, as he puts it elsewhere, being interested in it), then it could turn out that nonconscious organisms have interests. For, he emphasized, "the two senses really are logically distinct: A being can be interested in something that is not in his interests, and something may be in a being's interest despite the fact that he is not interested in it" (1976, p. 487). So it is possible for a being to have a good of its own without it being interested in anything, without it ever taking an interest in anything—that is, without it having any conscious desires at all.

Regan then argued that both plants and artifacts can coherently be said to have interests, because both can be good instances of their kind. True, he ad-

---

1. Or "lower animal." For simplicity's sake, I will usually speak of plants, but the arguments I advance in this chapter are intended to hold for all organisms that lack desires.

mitted, what qualities make a car a good car is ultimately a function of our interest in efficient transportation, yet

> a car has those characteristics it has, including those which are good-making, quite independently of our taking an interest in them. Cars do not *become*, say, comfortable or economical by becoming the objects of our interests. They are (or are not) comfortable or economical whether or not we have an interest in them, and whether or not we have an interest in their being comfortable or economical. (p. 493)

Similarly, he argued,

> A luxuriant gardenia, one with abundant blossoms and rich, deep green foliage is a *better gardenia* than one that is so deformed and stunted that it puts forth no blossoms at all, and this quite independently of the interests other beings happen to take in them. (p. 494)

Regan subsequently dismissed this argument as "completely muddled" (1981, p. 33). Although he did not explain the muddle, it can be brought out in the following way. A car, or even so simple an artifact as a can opener, can be said to need certain things, oil on its moving parts, for example, in order to be a good car or a good can opener, to be a good instance of its kind. However, such needs do not obviously correspond to interests of the car or the can opener. Even if Regan's argument established that a good car or a good can opener is intrinsically valuable (because they are good instances of their kinds), that would not suffice to show that cars or can openers can have interests—that is, a good of their own in the relevant sense. An analogy to art is useful here, since it sounds more plausible to say that a work of art is intrinsically valuable because of its beauty than it does to say that a car or a can opener is intrinsically valuable because it is a good instance of its kind. After all, a good thief is a good instance of his kind, but surely that does not suffice to show that a good thief is an intrinsically valuable thing. A beautiful work of art, however, can plausibly be claimed to be intrinsically good in virtue of its being beautiful. Yet a beautiful work of art has no good of its own, no interests, and this despite the fact that it can coherently be said to have various needs. For instance, a painting needs to be kept within certain temperature and humidity ranges if it is not to deteriorate and lose its beauty. But such needs do not define interests of the painting. Cars, can openers, and intrinsically valuable things all can coherently be said to have needs, but only things with a good of their own can coherently be said to have interests.

Regan's distinction between having an interest in something and taking an interest in it can still be used to motivate the question of whether nonconscious organisms can have interests, however. For about normal adult human beings we commonly say that they take no interest in what is nevertheless in their interest. As we noted at the outset of chapter 2, although every desire, taken in isolation, defines an interest of an animal that has desires, many things that are in our interest are never desired by us. For example, getting a certain amount of a given vitamin may be in my interest, despite the fact that I never take an interest in (form a desire for) getting enough of it. If things can be in our interests even when we never take any conscious interest in them, then perhaps things can be in plants' interests despite the fact that plants never take an interest in anything at all.

Whether or not this argument is convincing will depend ultimately on what we think defines the nonconscious interests of the paradigm possessors of interests: normal adult mammals. If all the nonconscious interests of mammals can be identified by reference to their desires—if not their actual desires, then the desires they would have under ideal conditions—then the fact that mammals sometimes do not actually desire things that are in their interests will not suggest that nonconscious organisms such as plants have any interests at all. On the other hand, if mammals have interests that cannot be identified by studying their desires—even the desires they would have under ideal conditions—then it may be that nonconscious organisms such as plants also have interests that can be defined in similar fashion. This will depend, of course, on what defines the nonconscious interests of mammals, but it may turn out that the same way of identifying these interests shows, when applied to plants, that they too have interests.

DIFFICULTIES FOR THE MENTAL STATE THEORY

It is fair to say that, at the present time, the dominant account of what is in a human being's interests fits the former, desire-based model. A common conception of individual welfare runs through such widely separated works as Henry Sidgwick's late-nineteenth-century classic, *The Methods of Ethics*, and John Rawls's late-twentieth-century classic, *A Theory of Justice*. On this conception of individual welfare, every actual desire generates an interest of the desiring person, but what is ultimately in a person's best interests, what is best for him all things considered, is defined by what his desires would be were he both (1) adequately informed and (2) impartial across phases of his life. As Sidgwick puts it,

> my "good on the whole" may be taken to mean what I should actually desire and seek if all the future aversions and desires, which would be roused in me by the consequences of seeking it, could be fully realized by me at the time of making my choice. (1893, p. 111; q.v. Rawls 1971, chap. 7, esp. pp. 407–16).

Let us call this the mental state theory of individual welfare (the mental state theory for short), because it embodies an attempt to identify everything that is in an individual's interests according to what the individual's desires are or would be under certain conditions.

The mental state theory has much to recommend it. First, it seems to imply the correct conclusions in a broad range of cases where we make judgments about what is in human beings' best interests, and the arguments we use to make such claims suggest that we are using something like the mental state theory in daily life. Appeals to what one's desires would be, if one were adequately informed and impartial across all phases of one's life, are commonly used to defend claims about what is in one's best interests. For example, parents respond to young George's refusal to eat his broccoli by arguing that he wants to grow up to be big and strong and that only by eating his broccoli will he be able to achieve this goal. In doing so, they are attempting to make George adequately informed about the implications of his own interests. If George still balks, then his parents react as if he is not being impartial across all phases of his life. They say he will be sorry and suggest that he is giving too much weight to his present desire not to eat broccoli: if he were impartial across all phases of his life, he would realize that as an adult he will wish he had grown up big and strong much more than he now wishes not to eat his broccoli.

The mental state theory is also parsimonious. It identifies all an individual's interests in the same way: by reference to his or her desires. However, if there are some cases in which references to desires (either actual or ideal) cannot adequately explain our judgments about what is good or bad for an individual, then clinging to it would represent not a laudable commitment to parsimony but dogmatism.

In this light, consider the case of Maude, an unusually intelligent and generally farsighted young adult who has a strong desire to smoke. Concerned for her welfare, we bring to her attention the fact that the best available evidence indicates that this smoking will shorten her life by a certain number of years. Suppose that Maude really takes this fact to heart, that the consequences of her conduct are accurately foreseen and adequately realized in her imagination at the present time, but that she nevertheless goes right on smoking. On the mental state theory, no sense can be made of the claim that Maude's smoking is bad for her—that is, that it is contrary to her interests. This is because she does not now desire to stop smoking, and on the mental state theory of harm this implies that continuing to smoke is bad for her only if her enlightened preference would be to stop smoking. But, by hypothesis, Maude is both adequately informed and impartial across all phases of her life. Therefore, her actual preference is her enlightened preference, and therefore, on the mental state theory of harm, Maude's smoking is in no way bad for her. But, surely, even if we were to admit that satisfying Maude's enlightened desire to smoke is ultimately in her best interests, there still some sense in which it is bad for her, completely independently of her desires. On the physiological level, it is bad for her lungs, and we presume that she has an interest in the proper functioning of all her organs, even if some other interest or constellation of interests ultimately overrides that interest. The mental state theory seems to be flawed in a fundamental way, because its major principle of identifying all interests with desires (actual or ideal) leaves out a familiar but fundamentally biological sense of what one's interests are.

Maude's is not an uncommon sort of case. The oddity of something bad turning out to be good derives from the circularity of the mental state theory: what a truly rational individual would choose under ideal circumstances is introduced to operationalize what one ought to desire, but then what a truly rational person would choose under ideal circumstances is surreptitiously limited by what the proponents of the mental state theory think one ought to desire. In *A Theory of the Good and the Right*, Richard Brandt offers a way out of this vicious circle. Brandt provides one of the most extensive and precise developments of some of the key notions in the mental state theory of individual welfare, and Brandt's analysis allows us to see how one could, in a noncircular way, deny that Maude's case is a possibility.

Brandt defines an "irrational desire" in psychological terms as "one that would extinguish after cognitive psychotherapy" (1979, p. 113). By "cognitive psychotherapy," he means repeated, vivid representation of available, relevant information. A's desire for X would extinguish after cognitive psychotherapy if and only if X's "valence" for A would be eliminated as a result—that is, if and only if A would cease to pursue X. Prior to introducing the notion of cognitive psychotherapy, Brandt (chap. 5) offers an account of pursuit and avoidance couched largely in noncognitive terms, in terms of classical conditioning. Brandt is then able to argue, not implausibly, that a desire like Maude's would be extinguished by cognitive psychotherapy. My hunch is that Brandt would treat Maude's overwhelming desire to smoke as a generalization from untypical examples or as an exaggerated valence produced by some early experience. If, for instance, Maude's life experience has been so traumatic that only reliance on nicotine has ever allowed her to feel that life is worth living, then it is understandable that she would rather smoke herself to death than live without cigarettes. It is not implausible to think that exposure to examples of how life can be worthwhile without cigarettes (through a creative stop-smoking program, for instance) would reduce the overwhelming valence smoking holds for her by establishing new associations between happiness and smoke-free existence.[2]

But the problem raised by Maude's case can be generated by reference to two less bizarre examples, where Brandt's noncircular specification of what it is rational to desire cannot help. Notice, first, that the mental state theory renders either meaningless or trivial many questions about the welfare of nonhuman animals. For example, does it make sense to ask, "Would my cat Nanci still desire access to the outdoors if she understood the risks involved?" Nanci clearly desires access to the outdoors, but she is presumably incapable of benefiting from the kind of cognitive psychotherapy Brandt advocates. Because nonhuman animals

2. Brandt does not discuss smoking specifically, but I draw here on his treatment of "Generalization from Untypical Examples" and "Exaggerated Valences Produced by Early Deprivation" (1979, pp. 120–26).

lack language, there is no way to represent vividly and repeatedly all the available information to them. I can imagine that, if Nanci suffered a frightful accident outside, she would subsequently want to stay inside all the time, but Nanci presumably is incapable of conceiving the many risks a cat faces outdoors. I doubt that she realizes that she gets fleas outside rather than inside the house (once she gets them, they are inside too—indeed, I have no evidence that she knows what a flea is) and I am certain she is incapable of understanding the risk of contracting FeLV (feline leukemia virus). So, with regard to these risks, there just is no relevant information by repeated and vivid representation of which we can change Nanci's desires. Given this and innumerable other questions about the welfare of animals, the mental state theorist has two options. The theorist could say that, because there is no way for us to present to the animal the relevant information we have, such questions are meaningless.[3] Or the theorist could say that, because the animals already have all the relevant information they are capable of considering, their actual desires decide the question. But surely this is incorrect. Whether or not access to the outdoors is in the best interests of a domestic cat is an important and legitimate question (I do not claim to have the definitive answer, but it is an important and legitimate question), and it is not to be answered simply by showing that the cat actually desires to go out.

There is another way of raising this problem for the mental state theory. Consider what the mental state theorist would have to say about the statement "Nineteenth-century mariners needed ten milligrams of ascorbic acid a day to avoid scurvy." Nineteenth-century mariners did desire to avoid scurvy, and they desired citrus fruit to that end. But nineteenth-century mariners knew no more about ascorbic acid than Nanci knows about FeLV. Brandt is quite explicit that the "available information" presented during cognitive psychotherapy is "the best justified system of beliefs *available at the time*," all the "relevant beliefs which are a part of the 'scientific knowledge' *of the day*" (1979, pp. 12, 112, emphasis added). But this means that even if it is now true that "nineteenth-century mariners needed ten milligrams of ascorbic acid a day to avoid scurvy," it wasn't true then. One could, of course, specify that the "available information" includes everything relevant from a completed or perfected human science. Given the revisability of actual scientific theories, this would be tantamount to assuming a godlike omniscience on the part of the cognitive psychotherapist. In any case, widening the "available information" would rob Brandt's appeal to cognitive psychotherapy its utility, of its being something you can actually do with people here and now.

3. Meaningless when asked about the cat's own best interests. The mental state theorist has no problem with the question, "Is Nanci's having access to the outdoors in Varner's best interests?" But my point here is that it is not just my welfare that is at stake, and it is when we ask the question about the cat that the mental state theory lets us down.

What has gone wrong with the mental state theory? At bottom, it is that desire contexts are referentially opaque, and consequently any attempt to define all of an individuals' interests in terms of desires (whether real or ideally adjusted) will run afoul of the fact that some attributions of needs are referentially transparent. That is, in talking about some of our interests—particularly those we label "needs"—substitution of coreferential expressions preserves truth value. For example, if it is in my interest to ingest at least ten milligrams of vitamin C daily, then it is also in my interest to ingest ten milligrams of ascorbic acid daily, because "ascorbic acid" and "vitamin C" are coreferential expressions—that is, they refer to exactly the same things. So, if vitamin C is good for me because it prevents scurvy, then so is ascorbic acid, because vitamin C is ascorbic acid. This is what is meant by saying that such need contexts are referentially transparent. When we talk about what a person wants or desires, rather than about what he needs, it is more plausible to say that statements about the interests in question can be made false by substitution of coreferential expressions—that is, such contexts are referentially opaque. Suppose, for instance, that I want to marry Nanci Griffith, the petite, unassuming folk singer-songwriter whose albums and concerts I adore. But suppose that, unbeknownst to me, her appearance and personality have been cleverly created by her record company, and Martha Mouth, my brash and portly neighbor, is actually the woman on the albums and in the concerts. While the sentence "Varner wants to marry Nanci Griffith" would be true, the sentence "Varner wants to marry Martha Mouth" would be false, despite the fact that Martha Mouth is Nanci Griffith. The mental state theory identifies all of our interests with (actual or ideal) desires, and substitution of coreferential terms in desire contexts does not always preserve truth value. So the mental state theory does not allow us to draw a distinction between a class of interests (such as the need to ingest ten milligrams of ascorbic acid daily) concerning which substitution of coreferential expressions preserves truth value and another class of interests (such as the desire to marry a person under a particular description or proper name) concerning which substitution of coreferential expressions does not preserve truth value (Thomson 1987, p. 101, makes a similar claim).

CHALLENGES FACING THE PSYCHO-BIOLOGICAL THEORY

In contrast to the mental state theory, if we were to define some of our interests—our "needs"—in terms of biological facts about us and the rest of our interests in terms of our desires, then we could say that, while substitution of coreferential expressions preserves truth value when we are talking about our needs (as in the example of vitamin C and ascorbic acid), substitution of coreferential expressions does not preserve truth value when we are talking about our desires (as in the Nanci Griffith–Martha Mouth example). Such an account would help us make sense of questions about what nineteenth-century mariners needed, independently of what they knew about their needs, just as it would help us make sense of questions about what is best for animals that are incapable of understanding much or all of what is relevant to the fulfillment of their needs. And it would allow us to say that Maude's continued smoking would still be in one sense bad for her, even if her desire survived cognitive psychotherapy.

Let us call this mixed account the psycho-biological theory of welfare, according to which to say that X is in A's interest means that

(1) A actually desires X,
(2) A would desire X if A were sufficiently informed and impartial across phases of A's life, or
(3) X serves some biologically based need that A has in virtue of being the kind of organism A is.

The *or* is inclusive, because sometimes one actually desires (sense 1) what one would desire after cognitive psychotherapy (sense 2), and what one desires also serves some biologically based need (sense 3). Not always, of course, but sometimes. This account handles all of the cases discussed in this chapter: before people knew anything about vitamins, before they could desire ascorbic acid, it was good for them in sense 3; whether or not my cat is capable of becoming better informed about them, certain things outdoors are hazardous to her health and thus potential harms in sense 3; and even if Maude's actual desire to smoke survived cognitive psychotherapy, it would still be bad for her in sense 3.

The discussion of Regan's response to Feinberg, with which I began this chapter, dramatizes the twin challenges that face any attempt to defend the biological portion (good in sense 3) of such a mixed theory of welfare. Because simple artifacts such as typewriters and cars clearly have needs in certain senses of the word, two things must be established before I can show how the fact that plants have needs suffices to show that they have interests. The first is empirical:

The empirical claim: plants have needs in some sense in which artifacts do not.

Unless this can be shown, the attempt to develop the psycho-biological theory of welfare will degenerate into a reductio ad absurdum: if identifying some of the interests of human beings with their biologically based needs implies that can openers and cars have interests, then surely we should abandon the biological portion of the psycho-biological theory of welfare. The second claim that must be defended is normative:

The normative claim: this difference between plants and artifacts qualifies plants, but not artifacts, for direct moral consideration.

To support the normative claim, one must show that the needs plants have are of a kind that suffices to give them direct moral standing.

Regan's remarks dramatize these twin challenges. But there is another challenge implicit in establishing the empirical claim, a problem that may have been in the back of Joel Feinberg's mind when he wrote a puzzling section of his seminal essay on "The Rights of Animals and Unborn Generations." Early in the essay, Feinberg appears to endorse a disjunctive criterion for the possession of interests. He says that a being can have interests only if it has conations, but under the concept of "conative life" he includes both "*conscious* wishes, desires, and hopes; or urges and impulses" and "*unconscious* drives, aims, and goals; or latent tendencies, direction[s] of growth, and natural fulfillments" (1974, pp. 49–50, emphasis added). In the section on plants, however, Feinberg insists that only *conscious* conations can define interests. Feinberg's insistence on drawing up the wagons around sentience has puzzled some commentators (see, for example, Goodpaster 1978, p. 320; Attfield 1981, pp. 39–40, and 1983, pp. 144–45). He gives very little by way of argument for abandoning the second disjunct of his earlier criterion. I suspect that a particular epistemological problem was troubling Feinberg when he wrote the section and that this, more than any argument he explicitly gives, explains his insistence on a sentience criterion for the possession of interests.

This interpretation explains what is otherwise a very puzzling remark in the "Vegetables" section of Feinberg's essay. Early in the section, Feinberg admits that "Plants . . . are not 'mere things'"; they are vital objects with inherited biological propensities determining their natural growth. . . . They grow and develop according to the laws of their own nature" (1974, pp. 51–52). Later in the section, however, he insists that "Plants may need things in order to discharge their functions, but their functions are assigned by human interests, not their own" (p. 54). Given that in the same paragraph he defines a thing's needs, in a morally neutral sense, as whatever is "necessary to the achievement of [its] goals, or to the performance of [its] functions" (p. 53), this is a very puzzling remark to make. If plants are "vital objects with inherited biological propensities," then why can it not be said that they have needs, at least in this morally neutral sense, quite independently of human interests in them?

Feinberg's puzzling remark, which I refer to as "Feinberg's dictum," has drawn a response from every author writing in defense of the claim that plants have interests. Yet most of that ink has been wasted, because most of these authors ignore an associated epistemological problem. What Feinberg may have meant to say, I suggest, is not that plants have no functions aside from those humans assign to them but rather that plants' functions cannot be specified on any other basis, and therefore any attempt to identify plants' interests with the fulfillment of their functions is doomed. The problem, in sum, is this:

The epistemological problem: even if plants have needs in some sense that artifacts do not, is it possible to specify, in a nonarbitrary way, what these needs are?

If we present Feinberg's dictum this way, then it becomes evident why certain responses commentators have made to his dictum fall very short of the mark.

In the remainder of this chapter, I first look at several of these responses and evaluate them simultaneously as responses to Feinberg's dictum and as responses to the epistemological problem. In the process, I identify and develop a response to Feinberg's dictum that simultaneously solves the epistemological problem and supports the empirical claim. However, this will not by itself establish the claim that plants have interests, that the needs in question are morally significant. After I argue that plants have needs in a sense in which artifacts do not, and provide a nonarbitrary criterion of what is and is not a need in this sense, I then show why the needs so described are morally significant, why they define interests of plants.

Supporting the Empirical Claim and Solving the Epistemological Problem

In a paper with the provocative title "Animal Chauvinism, Plant-Regarding Ethics, and the Torture of Trees," the aptly named J. L. Arbor says the following in response to Feinberg's dictum:

> it is clearly an error to put trees into the class of objects which have their ends determined outside themselves by conscious beings. Trees, like animals and other plants, but unlike machines, have end-states which are not decided by human beings. Given the right conditions and barring interference they will in the course of natural events reach this state. There is nothing mysterious or improper about insisting that whatever helps trees achieve their natural end-state is in their interest. (1986, p. 337)[4]

Arbor agrees with Feinberg that the "end-states" of artifacts are "decided by human beings" but insists that plants have "natural end-states."

---

4. Jon Moline once suggested to me that "J. L. Arbor" is too apt a name and that the paper was published under a pseudonym, presumably as a reductio ad absurdum of the biocentric individualist stance. I have not been able to confirm this hypothesis, but there is no other article by J. L. Arbor listed in *The Philosopher's Index*, there is no J. L. Arbor listed in the *International Directory of Philosophers*, and no academic affiliation is given at the end of Arbor's article. On the other hand, some Australasian environmental ethicists have intentionally changed their last names to reflect tree themes (Richard Sylvan and Val Plumwood, for example). So I don't know. If you're reading this, Mr. or Ms. Arbor, please drop me a note!

There is an initial air of plausibility to this claim. The view that there is one course of development that is "natural" for each species of organism (including all plants), in the sense that individuals of that species will inevitably develop along that course unless "external" factors "interfere," is a feature of popular consciousness. If shown two mature chestnut trees, for instance, a thin, gangly one living in a crowded woodlot and a massive, spreading specimen in an open field, we have a strong tendency to say that the latter is the "natural" state of a chestnut tree, and we expect a botanist to be able to explain why the gangly one has "failed" to develop "naturally."

However, Arbor's move fails as a response to Feinberg's dictum because it rests on an essentialist view of organic species that, as Elliott Sober details, is thoroughly discredited in modern biology. Essentialists treat variations within a species as deviations from "natural tendencies" caused by "interfering forces." The problem for biological essentialists is that, in light of modern biological theory, it is impossible to draw a nonarbitrary distinction between "natural tendencies" on the one hand and "interfering forces" on the other, so a stunted tree is as natural as a grand spreading chestnut.

In the first place, the natural tendencies of a species cannot be defined in terms of a specific genotype, because the genetic variability found among members of any given species—especially species that reproduce sexually—is staggering. But then also neither can the distinction be drawn in terms of the phenotypes that develop given a specific genotype. The problem, as Sober put it, is that

> when one looks to genetic theory for a conception of the relation between genotype and phenotype, one finds no such distinction between natural states and states which are the results of interference. One finds, instead, the *norm of reaction*, which graphs the different phenotypic results that a genotype can have in different environments. . . . Each of the [phenotypes] indicated in the norm of reaction is as "natural" as any other. (1980, p. 374)

This is why a botanist explains the chestnut trees' different "forms"—that is, their different phenotypes—in terms of such things as the effects of shading on the size and shape of understory trees rather than in terms of "interference" with a "natural" course of development.

A different response to Feinberg's dictum is offered by Paul Taylor in *Respect for Nature: A Theory of Environmental Ethics*:

> Though [many] machines are understandable as teleological systems . . . [t]he ends they are programmed to accomplish are not purposes of their own, independent of the human purposes for which they were made . . . [and] it is precisely this fact that separates them from living things. . . . The ends and purposes of machines are built into them by their human creators. It is the original purposes of humans that determine the structures and hence the teleological functions of those machines. . . . [A living thing] seeks its own ends in a way that is

not true of any teleologically structured mechanism. It is in terms of *its* goals that we can give teleological explanations of why it does what it does. We cannot do the same for machines, since any such explanation must ultimately refer to the goals their human producers had in mind when they made the machines. (1986, pp. 123–24)

Taylor claims that, while both plants and artifacts exhibit goal-directed behavior, the goals of artifacts cannot be identified without reference to the intentions of their human designers, whereas the goals of plants can be identified without reference to any human purpose, and that in this sense the goals of plants are their own in a way that goals of artifacts are not.

While Taylor's response to Feinberg is not biologically naive as is Arbor's, it is just as unconvincing. On any viable analysis of goal-directed behavior, Taylor's claim about the goals of artifacts is false. Certain artifacts are clearly goal directed, and their goals can be objectively specified quite independently of reference to any human purpose. Consider, for example, Ernest Nagel's paradigmatic analysis in *The Structure of Science.* Nagel argues that the

characteristic feature of such systems is that they continue to manifest a certain state or property G (or that they exhibit a persistence of development "in the direction" of attaining G) in the face of a relatively extensive class of changes in their external environments or in some of their internal parts—changes which, if not compensated for by internal modification in the system, would result in the disappearance of G (or in an altered direction of development of the systems). (1961, p. 411)

Although Nagel does not argue the point specifically, on his analysis it is true not only that "the distinctive features of goal-directed systems can be formulated without invoking purposes and goals as dynamic agents" (p. 418) but also that the goals of goal-directed artifacts can be identified without having ultimately to refer to the goals of their human producers or users.

For example, suppose that a team of alien scientists reaches Earth after a nuclear holocaust and discovers a supply of functional Patriot missiles in a Middle Eastern cave. With a little experimental ingenuity, they discover that the missiles intercept incoming projectiles. Not wanting to put a fine point on it, the scientist assigned to investigate the missiles tells the head scientist that "The missiles intercept incoming projectiles," or "The missiles turn in order to intercept incoming projectiles." Such explanations of the missiles' flight paths are teleological. Their goal has been accurately identified but without the scientists ever understanding a thing about contemporary aerial warfare. Moreover, it is not always the case that the "ends and purposes of machines are built into them by their human creators," as Taylor claims. If the Pentagon revealed that the inventor of the Patriot missile intended to build a ballistic missile for gathering weather data, that would not affect the accuracy of the foregoing explanation of its flight path, so long as the finished product in fact turns so as to intercept incoming projectiles.

Kenneth Goodpaster's response to Feinberg's dictum is similar to Taylor's, but, significantly, he speaks of "tasks" rather than "goals":

> As if it were human interests that assigned to trees the tasks of growth or maintenance! The interests at stake are clearly those of the living things themselves, not simply those of the owners or users or other human persons involved. (1978, p. 319)

The significance is this: insofar as Goodpaster is talking about biological functions rather than goals or end-states, it is possible to draw a sharp distinction between all artifacts, on the one hand, and all living organisms on the other. None of Feinberg's critics carefully distinguishes between ends, or goals, on the one hand and functions on the other. The reason may be simply that Feinberg fails to draw the distinction in his essay. Yet philosophers of biology have emphasized that a distinction must be drawn, and, once the distinction is made, a more promising approach to the empirical claim becomes obvious.

Although there is general agreement that functional claims in biology are grounded somehow in reproductive success leading to evolutionary development, it is clear that the functions of a given organism's organs or subsystems[5] cannot always be unpacked in terms of behavior directed to this goal. If they were, then statements such as "The function of a mule's eyes is to enable it to see" would be false. Mules are sterile. So if functional claims about individual organisms' organs were based on the reproductive fitness of the individual in question, mules' organs would have no functions.

In light of such considerations, the "standard line" (Allen and Bekoff 1994) among contemporary philosophers of biology has become an etiological account according to which biological functions are unpacked in terms of the evolutionary history of the organism's species. Although this account was pioneered by Larry Wright (1976), similar accounts have since been offered by Ruth Millikan (1984), Karen Neander (1991), and Fred Dretske (1995). Although there are differences in the details, on an etiological account:

X is a biological function of S (some organ or subsystem) in O (some organism) if and only if:

   (a) X is a consequence of O's having S and

   (b) O has S because achieving X was adaptive for O's ancestors.

---

5. Biological functions do not always (or even usually) attach to organs like the heart or lungs but rather to the systems (circulatory or respiratory) of which these organs form a part. Presumably, in single-celled organisms, biological functions attach to organelles or subsystems.

Such accounts are etiological because they make attributions of biological functions backward-looking to the etiology of the system in question. They are attractive to contemporary philosophers of biology, because they "naturalize" function attributions in a way that neatly overcomes the problem involving sterile organisms. Sight has been selected for in horses and in donkeys, and this is what explains the presence of eyeballs in the mule whether or not they contribute to the reproductive fitness of the mule.

For present purposes, what is most important about such analyses is that, with a modification of clause 3 in the psycho-biological theory, they provide us with a clear response to Feinberg's dictum and a clear answer to the epistemological problem. The theory then is that an individual *A* has an interest in *X* if and only if

(1) *A* actually desires *X*,

(2) *A* would desire *X* if *A* were adequately informed and impartial across phases of *A*'s life, or

(3) *X* would fulfill some biological function of some organ or subsystem of *A*, where *X* is a biological function of *S* in *A* if and only if

  (a) *X* is a consequence of *A*'s having *S* and

  (b) *A* has *S* because achieving *X* was adaptive for *A*'s ancestors.

This version of the psycho-biological account provides a clear answer to the epistemological problem, because what interests a given plant has on this account depends entirely on its species' etiology. Admittedly, a great deal of evolutionary research would have to go into giving a detailed and accurate answer to the question, "Exactly what is and is not in the interests of this plant?" But, on the view defended here, the answer to this question is objective, nonarbitrary, and—at least in principle—fairly precise and specific.

The proposed view also provides support for the empirical claim, because all and only living organisms are subject to natural selection. We can say that plants have needs in a sense in which artifacts do not, because plants' subsystems have biological functions but artifacts' subsystems do not. This is so despite the fact that most philosophers who have adopted an etiological account of biological functions have adopted similarly etiological accounts of artificial functions.

For example, Wright's generic analysis of functional explanations is that the function of a subsystem (whether biological or not) is "that particular consequence of its being where it is which explains why it is there" (1976, p. 81). For artifacts, the explanation of why it is there refers to conscious selection. The consequence of a floor-mounted headlight dimmer switch being where it is and having the form it has (its connections to the car's electrical system), which explains why it is there, is that it allows one to switch the headlights between high beam and low beam while driving. The designer consciously chose to put it there because its being there has this consequence. (The example is from Wright 1976, p. 77, n. 3, and pp. 79–80, n. 4.) Wright's claim is that attributions of biological functions began as useful but purely metaphorical attributions of analogous intentions to organisms, the metaphorical overtones of which were dropped once the theory of natural selection provided us with an alternative and nonmetaphorical way of filling in the "why" explanation. The consequence of woodpeckers' toes being where they are (in opposing pairs rather than in a 3/1 opposition as in perching birds), which explains why they are where they are, is that their being so arranged helps woodpeckers cling to the trunks of trees. Although no designer consciously chose to arrange them this way, this arrangement evolved because it is adaptive for organisms filling the woodpeckers' ecological niche.

One thing that distinguishes organisms from artifacts is that the former but not the latter are the result of natural selection. Why this should qualify the organisms and not the artifacts for direct moral consideration is the normative question, to which we turn in the following section. I will conclude this section with discussion of a related worry. Selective breeding of domesticated organisms might appear to constitute a difficult case for the view I am defending. For here, it might seem, what once were biological functions, determined by natural selection, are replaced by, or transformed into, artificial functions determined by human interests. This sort of worry begins to fade, however, as soon as we look at concrete examples.

In most cases, selective breeding does not alter the biological functions of any subsystem of the organism. Consider, for example, what selective breeding has done to the dairy cow. Today's heifers give more milk on less feed, but the selective breeding has not made it false that the (or at least a) biological function of the cows' mammary glands is to nourish their calves. The etiology of the species is still the same at the relevant point. Cows do not have mammary glands because milk fetches a profit for farmers; they have mammary glands because mammary glands produce the milk that sustains their calves. It is true that holsteins exist as a breed only because humans chose to breed them, but all that tells us is something about the function of the breed. It is true that there are holsteins only because heiffers who produce more milk fetch higher profits. So the function of this breed, in contrast to say herefords, is to produce milk in a way that fetches a profit. But that does not make it true that cows have mammary glands because milk fetches a profit. Not just cows but all female mammals have mammary glands, because females' suckling their young emerged as an adaptive strategy in a common ancestoral lineage. No amount of selective breeding will make it false that this is the (or at least a) biological function of mammary glands.

Selective breeding usually operates in this way: it alters some norm of reaction without thereby altering or eliminating any biological function. But now suppose that a strain of domestic turkey is produced with breast muscles so large that they cannot fly, like a powerlifter so muscle bound that he can no longer comb his hair. In such a case, I admit, these turkeys' breast muscles have lost their original biological function due to selective breeding. The capacity for flight is no longer a consequence of the turkeys' having breast muscles, and therefore condition (a) in the previously stated etiological account is no longer met. (This is how Wright 1976, pp. 89 and 91, treats all vestigial organs.) So selective breeding can affect the biological functions of an organism's subsystems. Moreover, in such a case, it is true that the breast muscles have in the process acquired an artificial function. Farmers' getting more profit out of each turkey is a consequence of the turkeys' having larger breast muscles, and the larger breast muscles are there precisely because farmers wanted more profitable turkeys.

In such a case, I admit, selective breeding has quite literally replaced the biological function of the breast muscles with an artificial function. But this is a very limited sort of case, and even here the organisms still have many subsystems with biological functions. It is still true, for example, that they have gizzards, stomachs, and intestines, because these organs result in their being nourished. It is therefore a mistake to conclude, in the case of the turkeys, that selective breeding has replaced all biological functions with artificial ones.

Only in one very limited kind of case will a living organism fail to have any biological functions. First mutations are problematic on an etiological account. In the first organism to have an adaptive mutation, there is no relevant etiology: this organism does not have the subsystem in question, because having it was adaptive for its ancestors. By hypothesis, this is the first organism with the trait. New traits acquire biological functions only via subsequent selective pressure (both Wright 1976 and Millikan 1984 treat first mutations this way). This implication of the etiological approach leads Christopher Boorse to object that, if a species "simply sprang into existence by an unparalleled saltation," then, on an etiological view, its organs would have no functions (1984, p. 373). However, for this to be literally true of an organism, it would have to have no ancestors, or at least share no nonvestigial organs or subsystems with its ancestors. Although it is possible that researchers will one day create a complete complement of DNA ex nihilo, all currently foreseeable DNA research either modifies one small portion of a given species' DNA or "splices" in genetic material from another organism, and in either case many biological functions are left unaffected.

So neither selective breeding nor currently foreseeable genetic research constitutes a significant challenge to the claim that all and only living organisms have biological interests, where these interests are identified with the fulfillment of the biological functions of their component subsystems and where these functions are in turn identified using a standard etiological account.

The psycho-biological theory provides us with answers to the empirical question and to the epistemological problem. All and only organisms have needs that are "natural"[6] in the sense of being defined by biological functions. No car or can opener has needs in this sense. And, pace Feinberg, it is in principle possible to specify, in a nonarbitrary way, what is and is not a need of this kind. It remains to be shown, however, that these are needs in a morally relevant sense. Why should we think that the biological functions of a plant's subsystems define interests? This is the normative question.

SUPPORTING THE NORMATIVE CLAIM

Several authors have offered arguments in support of the normative claim, but, while agreeing with the conclusion they reach (that nonconscious organisms have interests), I do not think their arguments make the strongest case that can be made for the normative claim. In this section, I survey several attempts to support the normative claim and show how the criticisms of the mental state theory of individual welfare offered in this chapter help make a stronger case.

After responding to Feinberg's dictum in the first section of "The Good of Trees," Robin Attfield asks us to imagine that the last sentient organism on Earth is a man who "hew[s] down with an axe the last tree of its kind, a hitherto healthy elm . . . which could propagate its kind if left unassaulted."[7] He concludes that

> Most people who face the question would . . . conclude that the world would be the poorer for this act of the "last man" and that it would be wrong. . . . And if, without being swayed by the interests of sentient creatures, we share in these conclusions and reactions, [then] we must also conclude that the interests of trees are of moral significance. (1981, p. 51)

A specific problem with Attfield's thought experiment is that it isn't clear why we must attribute interests to the tree in order to explain this intuition. Would most people still think it was wrong of the last man to chop down the tree if it were not the last of its kind? To the extent that peoples' intuitions change when the question is rephrased in this way, the explanation may be that they think the rarity of the tree makes it a thing of beauty and gives it some special moral significance, albeit of a different (and probably weaker) kind than it would have if it had interests. Lilly-Marlene Russow (1981) has argued, fairly convincingly, that aesthetic values drive the judgments people actually make about endangered

---

6. Obviously, "natural" is used differently in different contexts. There is more on this in chapter 6.

7. Attfield's example is flawed on empirical grounds. If the tree were indeed "the last of its kind," then it would be unable to reproduce, and even if it were heavy with viable seed at the time, the species would in all likelihood have already fallen below its minimum viable population. The example is nevertheless useful as a thought experiment.

species. Notice that Attfield himself says that people think "the world would be the poorer for this act of the 'last man,' " not that the tree itself would be harmed.

Apart from the specifics of Attfield's thought experiment, however, I doubt the utility of using appeals to intuitions about the morality of our treatment of plants to support the normative claim. Obviously, anyone who has already embraced biocentric individualism believes that plants have interests, and anyone who remains skeptical of the position doubts that they do. So the best defense of the normative claim that the needs of plants define interests would be one that begins from claims about human beings or closely related mammals. J. L. Arbor's defense of the normative claim therefore appears more promising than Attfield's "last man" argument.

Arbor asks us to imagine a society in which certain children are systematically mutilated in ways that normally would be quite painful but only after brain surgery has left them incapable of feeling the pain and unhappiness that would otherwise attend these operations and mutilations. Arbor concludes that to unpack the "wrong" done to these children as a violation of an indirect duty to other, normal children and adults would be "an artificial and awkward way of responding to a straightforward ethical intuition" (1986, p. 338).

While Arbor's approach is more promising than Attfield's, it does not provide the strongest possible defense of the normative claim, because perfectly good sense can be made of the claim that direct duties to the children are being violated in this case, without abandoning a sentience criterion of moral considerability. A sentientist need only appeal to the loss of potential positive experiences of pleasure or desire satisfaction to claim that the children have been harmed. A sentientist can say that these children have been made drastically less well off than they would otherwise have been and that they have in that sense been seriously harmed.

I therefore believe that Kenneth Goodpaster is on the right track when he suggests that allegiance to a hedonistic theory of individual welfare is responsible for the general reluctance of Western philosophers to recognize the moral considerability of nonsentient organisms. Goodpaster observes:

> Though [the concept of morality] is not *exhausted* by its inclusion of reference to the *good* and *harm* done to others by an agent, this reference is surely a central part of it. Beneficence and nonmaleficence, then, are not only necessary ingredients in our shared conception of moral (vs. nonmoral) obligation, they are *central*. But one cannot do good for or avoid harm to entities that have no interests. (1980, p. 282)

Given that only entities capable of being benefited and harmed can be the objects of direct duties of beneficence and nonmaleficence, the general allegiance of Western authors to a hedonistic conception of individual welfare explains their reluctance to recognize the moral considerability of nonsentient organisms (Goodpaster 1978, pp. 320–22). However, there are two problems with Goodpaster's argument, problems that seriously weaken it as a defense of the normative claim.

The first problem is that Goodpaster offers no specific argument against the adequacy of a hedonistic conception of welfare and in favor of a nonsentientist conception. Goodpaster appears to presume that, by offering support for the empirical claim, he is simultaneously offering support for the normative claim. Without an argument connecting the two, the normative claim is very weakly supported, because no argument has been offered for thinking that the alternative, nonsentientist conception of welfare is superior to the hedonistic conception.

The second problem is that, in characterizing as "hedonistic" the dominant theory of individual welfare, Goodpaster casts his net too narrowly. As noted at the beginning of this chapter, in the dominant theory of individual welfare, an individual's interests are defined in terms of desires rather than pleasure and pain simpliciter: anything an individual actually desires defines one of that individual's interests, but whatever an individual would desire if adequately informed and impartial across all phases of that individual's life is in that individual's best interests. Since it would be more plausible to say that this, rather than a narrowly hedonistic conception of welfare, is the dominant conception in contemporary Western philosophy, the strongest defense of the normative claim would be one that called it into question rather than the hedonistic conception.

This is precisely what I do in the arguments presented in this chapter concerning Maude's smoking, the sailors' need for ascorbic acid, the cat's desire to go outside, and my desire to marry Nanci Griffith (above, pp. 58–61). These arguments show that the mental state theory of individual welfare is inferior to a psycho-biological account that includes, as part of the definition of the interests of humans and other mammals, a biology-based account of needs. The specific account developed in the preceding section is one such account. It allows one to recognize a distinction between two kinds of interests, those that are relativized to the beliefs of an individual (such as the desire to marry someone) and those that are not (such as the need to maintain functional lungs or the need for ascorbic acid). The examples involving the cat's desire to go outside and the mariners' need for ascorbic acid lead us, in light of the account offered in the preceding section, to the conclusion that the fulfillment of the biological functions of the organs and subsystems of our bodies is in our interests, not just irrespective of our actually taking a conscious interest in their fulfillment, but even irrespective of our being capable of consciously taking an interest in their fulfillment. But if the fulfillment of the biological functions of our subsystems is in our interest irrespective of our even being capable of consciously taking an interest in their fulfillment, would not the fulfillment of those functions in plants be in their interest, even though they are incapable of taking an interest in them? That is the best available argument for the expansive conception of moral standing represented in biocentric individualism.

Individuating Organisms That Do Not Have Desires

I argue above that every living organism has an interest in the fulfillment of the biological function of each of its component organs and subsystems, and I show that an etiological conception of biological functions allows one to say, in a nonarbitrary and—at least in principle—a fairly specific way, what these biological interests are. I say "in principle," because in practice very detailed knowledge of a species' phylogeny would be necessary in order to say in any exhaustive way what biological interests its individual members have. Probably the relevant research has not been done for any particular species, and certainly it is not a philosopher's task to do it. But, even if the relevant research had already been done, some philosophical and conceptual puzzles would remain.

One of these is the puzzle of whether and how to individuate asexually reproducing organisms. Teddybear cholla flower and reproduce sexually, but more often than not they reproduce asexually by budding: their "joints" break off easily when brushed against by an animal, and these joints fall to the ground or are carried some distance by the animal (their spines are barbed) before sprouting. The puzzle is, when a teddybear cholla (or other asexually reproducing organism) reproduces by budding, do we suddenly have two individuals, and two sets of interests, where before we had only one?

This would seem to be a crucial question for a biocentric individualist. Teddybear Pass in Organ Pipe Cactus National Monument is covered with thousands of cholla—but are these thousands of individuals or only a few? All the navel oranges in the world have been reproduced from a few mutant individuals—but are there tens of thousands of these trees or just a few? If the sheer number of biological interests at stake mattered greatly, and more individuals meant more interests at stake, then the answer to this question would be momentous. However, for the reasons given in the following chapter, I do not think it matters much how we answer this question. I am comfortable with a rather decadent ontology of interests, because the principles I advance in chapter 4 for adjudicating conflicts are insensitive to the numbers of interests involved.

Nevertheless, the question of individuation is of independent philosophical interest, and so I conclude this chapter by considering it briefly. Some with whom I have discussed this puzzle say that any part of an organism that is detached and thrives elsewhere constitutes a separate organism with its own biological interests. I prefer to say that clonal reproduction never results in more than one individual, it just results in the one individual having noncontiguous parts. Consider an aspen grove where what appear to be many separate trees are actually connected below ground. This is one tree. Its roots have sprouted many trunks, but it is every bit as much one tree as a live oak that splits into several main branches just above the ground. Now suppose we sever the connection between the roots underlying one trunk and those underlying the others. Here it seems to me that we still have one tree, even though one of its parts is no longer connected to the rest. I do not see how it makes any difference if we then move the severed part far away. Nor do I see that it makes any difference if initially the severed part lacks some of the organs or subsystems necessary for survival—for example, when we take a cutting from an orange tree. If the severed part regenerates the relevant organs or subsystems wherever it is planted, then I think we just have one organism with parts thriving in two locations.

Those who favor the other answer (that thriving parts are individuals with interests of their own) have tended to appeal to examples involving animals. For example, they say, suppose I split an earthworm asunder and throw the halves into different compost piles. If each regenerates its missing parts and thrives, then it is tempting to say that we now have two individuals where before we had only one. Admittedly, I am initially hesitant to treat the worm analogously to the plants, but that hesitance is, I think, due to the fact that the "animals" we are most used to thinking about and dealing with are the "higher" vertebrates (mammals and birds). Once we understand the implications of this bias, the oddity of speaking of one earthworm thriving simultaneously in two compost piles is at least attenuated.

Part of the oddity is due to the fact that we are not used to thinking of animals' parts as separable at all. The animals we are most used to dealing with are the highly differentiated vertebrates, whose severed legs and heads do not continue to function. So when both halves of the worm continue to function, we tend to assume that a whole new individual has come into existence, as we would expect if a severed human hand or dog's leg were to regenerate the rest of a body. But there is nothing inconceivable in the notion of an animal's parts being separable, and our reason for supposing that a severed leg that regenerated a body would constitute a different individual involves mental attributes that are presumably inapplicable to an earthworm.

To see how a single animal's parts could function in different locations, suppose that, instead of being connected to my brain by long networks of nerves, the muscles in my hands were operated by a kind of natural radio signal. Then I could detach my arms and go down the hall to check my mailbox without leaving off typing (assuming, of course, that I could remove my arms without bleeding to death and that I am a touch typist!).

When the severed worm prospers simultaneously in two compost piles, it is more like a person leaving his hands at the keyboard than a severed dog's leg developing a new body. In the latter case, we are confident that the result is a new individual because the new dog's memories and desires will be different from the old dog's. When it comes to the "higher" vertebrates, we distinguish individuals on the basis of mental properties as much as on the basis of physical properties; we are prepared to entertain mind–body transfers, brains in vats, and so on, because here the individual is more closely identified with certain memories and desires than with a certain body type. But in the case of the earthworm, these mental properties presumably are missing altogether. An earthworm presumably has no conscious memories or desires, and therefore this way of determining which individual is the original one is inapplicable. In the case of a human being or a dog, if a severed appendage regenerated the rest of a body, the original individual would be the one that, because it retained the original brain, retained the original memories and desires (or at least some kind of continuity with these). But, since the earthworm has no memories or desires on the basis of which we could differentiate the "old" individual from the "new" one, the only answer we can give to the question, "Which half of the earthworm is the original individual?" is: both! What we have here, as in the case of the cholla cactus or the navel orange, is one individual whose parts are now thriving in different locations. Here again, because the "animals" we are most used to thinking about and dealing with are the "higher" vertebrates, I think that we are led to say inappropriate things about the earthworm.

Although I prefer to speak of the numerous clones of plants and lower animals being all one individual with parts in different places, I think that nothing of ethical substance hangs on this issue. In the next chapter, I develop a variant of Ralph Barton Perry's principle of inclusiveness and modify it for application to a broader range of cases than Perry intended. The modification ensures wide applicability, but it also makes the number of interests involved irrelevant. Where certain desires of human beings are at odds with the biological interests of nonconscious organisms such as cholla cactus, aspen, navel oranges, or earthworms, it does not matter how many of those nonconscious individuals there are. In this respect, the view I adopt resembles a rights-based ethics: the numbers do not count.

CHAPTER FOUR

The Principle of Inclusiveness

Establishing Priorities among Interests

THE SATISFACTION of interests constitutes a fundamental moral value, because to say that a being has interests is to say that it has a welfare, or good of its own, that matters from the moral point of view. So if an action would satisfy an interest, that is a prima facie reason for performing it. On the other hand, the dissatisfaction of interests constitutes a fundamental moral disvalue. So if what I do sets back the interests of some other being, that is a prima facie reason for not doing it.

This poses a problem for my view, because in chapters 2 and 3 an enormous range of interests is identified: the desires[1] of at least all normal adult mammals and birds (and perhaps also reptiles, amphibians, and a few invertebrates) and the biological interests of all living things. But if every living organism has interests, then it is impossible to avoid thwarting innumerable interests of others. As John Passmore put it in the first book-length treatment of environmental ethics,

> the Jainist principle [of avoiding harm to all living things] . . . is far too strong. This is the more obvious now that we are aware of the minute living organisms which everywhere surround us. In breathing, in drinking, in eating, in excreting, we kill. We kill by remaining alive. (1974, p. 123)

In the intervening years, Baird Callicott has gone further to assert that the sheer multitude of interests recognized by biocentric individualism makes the stance untenable. In his "Search for an Environmental Ethic," a narrative bibliography of work in the field, he begins with anthropocentrism and continues through extensionism to holism to argue that, besides having environmentally unsound implications, extensionist views are fundamentally impracticable:

1. As I am using the term in this book, an interest is, by definition, morally significant. From here on, I speak interchangeably of "desires" and "interests defined by desires." The latter is more precise, because a desire is not by definition morally significant. However, the former way of speaking is much more economical and will not, I trust, occasion any misunderstanding.

> An equitable system for resolving conflicts of interests among individuals is a
> reasonable, *practicable* goal if the individuals whose interests are to be equally
> considered are relatively few and far between. . . . [But] when every living thing
> is extended moral considerability, then the *practicability* quotient approaches
> zero; a point of moral overload is reached and the whole enterprise of ethics
> threatens to collapse into absurdity. (1986, pp. 402–3)

Whereas Passmore worries that the extension of moral standing to all living
organisms threatens to make the basic act of living immoral, Callicott suspects
that the extension will cause a kind of cognitive overload, making it impossible
to give adequate consideration to all of the interests that are at stake in most
situations.

My goal in this chapter is to show that both are wrong, that Passmore's
worry can be allieviated in a way that simultaneously allays Callicott's suspicion.
I do so by appealing to a simple and—at least in its original form—almost wholly
unobjectionable principle, Ralph Barton Perry's principle of inclusiveness. I use
Perry's principle to defend the following principle:

(P1) Generally speaking, the death of an entity that has desires is a worse
thing than the death of an entity that does not.

This principle expresses a priority-of-desires view. Once established, it solves
Passmore's worry. Starving myself to death would frustrate many of my desires.
Many other animals also have desires that would be set back were they to die,
but plants (and some "lower" animals) do not. Principle P1 therefore implies
that I should eat these desireless creatures rather than starve (and, similarly, that
I should not quit breathing or defecating, to save some microorganisms). Principle P1 also shows how easily Callicott's suspicion about cognitive overload can
be allayed. Callicott's worry is that the sheer number of interested beings recognized by a biocentric individualist position makes it impossible to deal with
all the relevant considerations. But an analogy shows why this need not be so.
Suppose I want to read something about edible landscaping and I walk into a
large bookstore to find an appropriate book. I do not stop and examine each
book I find—I would never get beyond the sale bin at the front if I did!—I go
straight to the home and garden section. The fact that there are so many books
on so many subjects in the store is no problem. I can easily avoid most of them
because I know ahead of time what subject I am interested in, and the books are
clearly labeled by subject. Analogously, the difference between entities with desires (mainly vertebrates) and those without desires, including plants and microorganisms, is as clear as the labels in the bookstore. Admittedly there are bor-
derline cases, but, given that no plant or microorganism has desires, deciding
what to eat from my kitchen in light of P1 is as easy as deciding where in the
bookstore to look for a book on edible landscaping: I know to eat the rutabaga
rather than my cat just as I know to go to the gardening section rather than the

philosophy section in the bookstore. Passmore's worry can be alleviated if certain general priorities can be established among various broad categories of interests, and doing so simultaneously saves biocentric individualism from the cognitive overload that Callicott foresees.

I argue for the priority of desires over biological interests but also for the priority of certain human desires over the desires of animals. Donald VanDeVeer observes that Peter Singer "lost some hard-won credibility" when he suggested that a situation in which rats are biting ghetto children involves a genuine conflict of interest (1979, p. 55). What seems incredible about Singer's suggestion is not the claim that rats have interests (that position had achieved credibility) but his claim that any conflict that exists between the rats' interests and the humans' interests in such a case is "genuine." Singer's suggestion that the conflict is "genuine" implies that the interests at stake are pretty evenly balanced or that it is a difficult case to decide, but people such as VanDeVeer, who are moved by Singer's analyses of factory farming and experimentation, still find no difficulty resolving the case involving the rats. To make the extension of moral standing to nonhuman animals plausible, one must give priority to at least some human interests over the interests of animals. That is, in addition to a principle like P1, a principle somewhat like P2 must be defended:

(P2) The satisfaction of the desires of humans is more important than the satisfaction of the desires of animals.

The suggested principles threaten to be too permissive, however; the attempt to make biocentric individualism plausible threatens to trivialize it. This is obvious in the case of P2, which would appear to grant human beings carte blanche over the lives of animals by suggesting that the most trivial of human desires can override all of an animal's desires. But this is implausible. If the alternative were starvation, I would presumably be justified in eating my cat, but surely my desire to see the cat fry does not justify my microwaving it. I defend biocentric individualism against charges of triviality by using the principle of inclusiveness to defend a weaker version of P2, namely P2':

(P2') Generally speaking, the satisfaction of ground projects is more important than the satisfaction of noncategorical desires.

This principle expresses a priority-of-ground-projects view. The terms "ground project" and "categorical desire" are defined more carefully below, but in short these terms refer to the most inclusive of all interests, interests that only human beings (and, perhaps, a very few other higher mammals) have. Once established, this principle alleviates VanDeVeer's worry without trivializing the biocentric individualist stance. Principle P2' does not give humans carte blanche to use animals in any way we like, but it does imply that, where our most important interests are at stake, we can use animals in various ways. Microwaving my cat cannot plausibly be said to further my most inclusive interests, but if there were literally nothing else for me to eat, P2' implies that I would be justified in eating my cat.

In chapter 6, I respond to the larger charge that the emphasis on human desires in P2' has environmentally unsound consequences. However, P1 has its own problems. First, to say that desires take precedence over biological interests would seem to imply that, if only I could remove all desiring creatures first, I would be justified in torching old-growth forest (as Mary Midgley [1983] once put it) just "to see how all would burn." Second, to say that desires take precedence over biological interests would seem to imply that overpopulated animals should be fed rather than culled, to the detriment of natural ecosystems. Chapter 5 includes a response to this kind of worry about P1 in the context of a general consideration of the implications of animal rights views for environmental policy. My defense of P1 in the present chapter includes discussion of the former problem. I conclude this chapter with a brief response to a third apparent problem with P1, that it would seem to elevate an individual's most trivial desires above that individual's putatively more important biological interests, making (for example) Maude's desire to smoke more important than her biological interest in the continued functioning of her lungs.

Perry's Principle of Inclusiveness

In his *General Theory of Value*, Ralph Barton Perry introduces the principle (or, as he often refers to it, the standard) of inclusiveness in the following way:

> The standard of inclusiveness may . . . be expressed as follows. If an interest M confers value on its object a, and if a second interest N confers value on the same object, the interest M persisting, it follows that a derives augmented value from this fact. Or if a *is* the object of the favorable regard of both M and N, and if either of these interests be withdrawn leaving the other, there will then be a loss of value, although a will still retain value owing to the remaining interest. (1926, p. 647)

Perry emphasizes the deep beauty of this principle: it eliminates the need for any direct measure of the relative value of various interests' satisfaction or dissatisfaction. It eliminates the need, as he put it, to assign any "comparative magnitude" to the satisfaction of interests (p. 654). By a "comparative magnitude," Perry means a measure of cardinal as opposed to ordinal utility—that is, a measure of any aspect of an interest that can be assigned a number and then added, subtracted, multiplied, or divided with other comparative magnitudes to say that the disvalue created by setting back one interest is made up for by the value created by another interest's satisfaction.

The prospects for assigning cardinal utilities to the satisfaction of various interests are dim for several reasons. First, and most obvious, it certainly will not do to say that all interests are on a par, morally speaking—that is, that the more interests satisfied the better. For suppose that only three interests are at stake (A, B, and C) in two possible outcomes, (i) and (ii):

(i) A and B are satisfied while c goes unsatisfied.
(ii) C is satisfied while both A and B go unsatisfied.

If A and B are what seem intuitively to be very trivial interests (such as that defined by the desire to achieve a consistent number of rotations while flipping a coin) while C is what seems intuitively to be a very important interest (such as one's biological interest in adequate nutrition or one's desire to succeed professionally), then it would be wildly implausible to say that outcome (i) would be better than outcome (ii). We cannot compare states of affairs or the actions that bring them about by simply comparing the total numbers of interests satisfied in each state of affairs. There is a sense in which more interests being satisfied is always better, but this is not it. It is not true that a greater number of interests being satisfied (both A and B) is always better than a smaller number of interests being satisfied (just C).

If the intensity and duration of pleasure and pain were reliable measures of the satisfaction and frustration of interests, then there would be some hope of assigning cardinal utilities to the satisfaction of various interests and using these measures to augment our intuitive judgments. Then it would be possible, at least in principle, to compare the intensity and duration of various pleasures and pains in various species. The pain and stress a calf in a confinement veal operation experiences during its lifetime could be compared to the intensity and duration of the pleasure experienced by the connoisseurs who consume its anemic flesh, and the pleasure Nanci feels while prowling outside or while eating the treat for which she returns to the house could be compared to the intensity and duration of the pleasure I feel while working on this book or while eating my favorite stir-fry. But feelings of pleasure and pain are not reliably correlated with the satisfaction or frustration of interests, for two reasons. First and foremost, nonconscious organisms such as plants have interests whose satisfaction creates value without creating any pleasure (or preventing any pain). And, second, even among sentient animals pleasure need not accompany the satisfaction of a desire (writing this book has at some points been pure hell) nor pain the frustration of a desire (I will never experience pain or distress because my idle wish to become a great acoustic guitarist will never be satisfied).

Nor is the intensity of an interest a reliable guide to the cardinal utility of its satisfaction. In the case of interests defined by desires, "intensity" naturally enough refers to the consciously felt urgency of the desire: one's more intense desires are those that absorb one's conscious attention. Where entities without desires are concerned, felt urgency cannot serve as a measure of intensity, but a parallel criterion would be the degree to which a biological interest "has acquired command of the body as a whole" (Perry 1926, p. 629). Perry suggests this as the measure of an interest's "intensity." While he does not recognize the existence of biological interests, his criterion can perhaps be applied to entities that do not have desires, including those (like plants) that do not literally "behave" at all.

> Despite our ignorance of the physiological terms in which intensity of interest should be expressed, we can conceive of it in abstract terms as a quantity of a certain type. It is a ratio of the elements which are acting under the control of the interest, to the totality of the elements of the organism. (p. 630)

But in neither of these senses is intensity a reliable guide to the relative importance of the satisfaction of various interests. The interests that most absorb one's attention or command one's body are not necessarily—and perhaps not even usually—the most important interests of the individual or the most important interests from a moral point of view. An alcoholic thinks more about alcohol than good nutrition or career, and it is quite literally true that alcohol "acquires command of an alcoholic's body as a whole." Similarly, a biological interest sometimes acquires complete control over the body of an insect or plant in a way that leads to self-destruction, as when a male preying mantis pursues sex only to be eaten by his female partner.

Another difficulty with assigning cardinal utilities to various interests' satisfaction is that it is an oversimplification to speak of interests as being either "satisfied" or "unsatisfied." In *Harm to Others*, Joel Feinberg points out that we have a surprisingly rich and nuanced vocabulary for describing setbacks to interests. We speak variously of

1. "defeating" an interest, in which an interest is "put to utter rout, . . . conclusively and irrevocably [set back]";
2. "dooming" an interest, which means to "foreordain its defeat," whether this is known to the victim or not;
3. "setting back" an interest, in which the stress is on the "reverse [of] its progress";
4. "impeding" an interest, which is "to slow its advancement without necessarily stopping or reversing it, to hinder or delay";
5. "thwarting" an interest, which means "to stop its progress without necessarily putting it in reverse"; and
6. "violating" an interest, which implies that, in addition to being harmed, the victim has also been wronged, so that "only persons acting improperly 'violate' interests." (1984, pp. 51–55)

Following Feinberg's lead, we can also distinguish among various types or degrees of the satisfaction of interests:

7. "satisfaction" of an interest, whether temporary or final;
8. "final satisfaction" of an interest, in which it is satisfied "conclusively and irrevocably";
9. "ongoing satisfaction" of interests that do not or cannot achieve final satisfaction;
10. "temporary satisfaction," in which an interest is satisfied at some point in time without its ongoing satisfaction being guaranteed indefinitely;
11. "ensuring" or "safeguarding" the ongoing satisfaction of an interest;
12. "foreordaining the final satisfaction of an interest"; and
13. "furthering" an interest, in which the stress is on "furthering its progress" without necessarily ensuring its final satisfaction.

So not only is there a bewildering variety of interests, there is a bewildering variety of ways and degrees of satisfaction and dissatisfaction of interests.

A related complication is introduced by the fact that, while some of our interests are episodic, others are persistent, and it is unclear how to compare the satisfactions of the two. The paradigm cases of episodic interests are those that come into existence at a fairly specific time and are decisively satisfied or defeated in relatively short order. Other interests are more persistent, meaning that they are with us for a long time (sometimes our whole lives) and we speak of them as being relatively satisfied or set back at various points in time. A biological interest in good nutrition is an example of the latter. Such an interest is with us from the cradle to the grave and is never satisfied or defeated once and for all (except at death)—it is more or less fully satisfied at each moment in time. The desire to see a cedar waxwing this winter would define a relatively episodic interest. I formed it on an October morning over coffee, looking at my backyard, and by spring it was either satisfied or defeated. If my interest in good nutrition is with me from the cradle to the grave, does its satisfaction through time count just once, whereas the desire to see a waxwing this winter counts repeatedly because I can re-form it each fall? Or does my interest in good nutrition create more value the longer it is satisfied, so that the continued satisfaction of a persistent interest can outweigh the serial satisfaction of episodic interests?

For the foregoing reasons, the prospects for assigning cardinal utilities to the satisfaction of various interests appear to be pretty grim, but that is precisely what makes the principle of inclusiveness so attractive. Perry argued that, because it compares the value created by the satisfaction of a set of interests to that created by the satisfaction of a proper subset of those same interests, the principle can be applied independently of any measure of comparative magnitudes: "The whole is greater than its part because it contains the part, *and* something besides; thus

exceeding the part, *whatever otherwise be the magnitude of either whole or part"*
(1926, p. 646).

Perry's formulation of the principle of inclusiveness can be formalized as
follows: it is always better to satisfy all of the interests in a given set rather than
any proper subset of that same set. So formulated, the principle is wholly unobjectionable, providing we make two assumptions:

(A1) The satisfaction of any interest is, considered in and of itself, a good
thing (and the dissatisfaction of any interest is, in and of itself, a bad
thing), and

(A2) Only the satisfaction or dissatisfaction of interests matters from the
moral point of view.

I endorse A2, at least for the purpose of this book. My purpose in this book is
not so much to prove biocentric individualism and defend it against all rivals but
rather to articulate the biocentric individualist stance more fully than it has been
before and, in the process, to defend it against the objection that it is antienvironmental. My own view is that the jury is still out on the question of pluralism,
but, for the purposes of this book, I assume that nothing but the satisfaction and
dissatisfaction of interests matters from the moral point of view.

In making the other assumption (that the satisfaction of any interest, in and
of itself, is always a good thing) I am not denying that there are inherently evil
interests. Consider, for instance, the desire to set back as many interests of others
as possible, even where there is no benefit to oneself (aside from the satisfaction
of this twisted desire). This, I take it, would be an inherently evil desire in the
sense that it is the direct opposite of the desire to be morally good (at least under
assumption A2). That being said, I still maintain that the satisfaction of such a
desire would be a good thing, as long as the desire could be satisfied without the
desired result actually occurring. Suppose that the person with this desire was
the solitary creature in James's imagined world. I think it would be a good thing
if this person's desire could be satisfied by a complicated hallucination. Such a
desire would still be inherently evil, in the sense that it expresses a desire to be
morally evil, but its satisfaction would still be a good thing, as long as it could
be satisfied without actually setting back any other interests.

It might be claimed that this is not possible, however. Perhaps a desire for
something to happen is always the desire to have it actually happen. But, as we
saw in the previous chapter, desire contexts are referentially opaque, and for this
reason it is possible to satisfy a desire that something happen without it actually
happening. A biological interest cannot be satisfied without the fulfillment of the
biological function of the subsystem in question, but if I believe that something
has happened, then my desire that it happen is satisfied (at least until I revise my
beliefs).

The satisfaction of a more sophisticated desire, the desire to have it actually be the case that one sets back as many interests of others as possible, would be a bad thing. Such a desire is inherently evil in an additional sense, namely that its satisfaction would necessarily involve not just evil but thoroughgoing or pervasive evil. Many biological interests are such that their satisfaction requires the defeat of other interests. For instance, ensuring the satisfaction of my biological interest in the functioning of my lungs requires the deaths, and therefore the defeat of the interests of, millions of disease microorganisms that are continually invading my lungs. The satisfaction of this interest involves an evil (on the view defended in chapter 3, the death of these microorganisms is an evil because it dooms all their interests), but satisfying the desire to actually set back as many interests of others as possible would involve thoroughgoing or pervasive evil. It is an inherently evil desire both insofar as it is the very opposite of the desire to be good and insofar as its satisfaction would involve thoroughgoing or pervasive evil. I do not know how far from the desire to be good a desire must be, or how pervasive the evil required by an interest's satisfaction must be, for it to be fairly labeled an inherently evil interest, but the desire to actually defeat as many interests of others as possible can serve as a paradigm, and the closer an interest approximates this desire, the more clearly it is inherently evil.

Another implication of assumption A1 is that events as well as actions can be evaluated in moral terms. The interests of plants and animals are affected not only by the actions of moral agents and the policies adopted by agents acting in concert (politically) but also by events that happen independently of human beings. A hurricane that rips through a barrier island sets back the interests of the trees it uproots and the animals it drowns, making the situation afterward objectively worse than before. The hurricane is not a moral agent, and so we would not say that it wrongs the animals it kills or that the occurrence of the hurricane is an injustice. Still, in terms of the satisfaction of interests, the island's devastation is a moral evil. So I restrict the use of the terms "right" and "wrong" and "justice" and "injustice" to descriptions of the actions of moral agents singly or in concert; but I use the terms "good" and "bad," "better" and "worse," and so on more generally to describe not only actions but also nonanthropogenic states of affairs and events.

Under assumptions A1 and A2, Perry's principle of inclusiveness is wholly unobjectionable. However, the principle's application is severely limited, as Perry takes pains to emphasize:

> There is a fundamental characteristic of the principle of inclusiveness which must be held clearly in mind. . . . This principle is applicable only to interests or aggregates of interests that are related as *whole and part*. The whole is greater than its part because it contains the part, *and* something besides; thus exceeding the part, *whatever otherwise be the magnitude of either whole or part*. The determi-

nation of comparative inclusiveness depends on the possibility of superimposition and overlapping.

It is impossible for the same reason to judge by the method of inclusiveness between the objects of two *conflicting* interests. (1926, p. 646)

Where it is impossible to satisfy two interests simultaneously, Perry's restriction renders the principle of inclusiveness inapplicable.

Yet Perry himself abandons this restriction, at least implicitly, during his treatment of William James's "lost soul" example. In "The Moral Philosopher and the Moral Life," James asks us to imagine

> a world in which Messrs. Fourier's and Bellamy's and Morris's utopias should be all outdone, and millions kept permanently happy on the one simple condition that a certain lost soul on the far-off edge of things should lead a life of lonely torture. (Quoted in Perry 1926, p. 670.)

Perry says that, in light of the problem of assigning cardinal utilities ("comparative magnitudes") to the satisfaction of various interests, there is "no solution of the problem through a comparative judgement *between* the lost soul and the happy millions." Nevertheless, he argues, "The answer seems clear. We are impelled to go out to that lonely sufferer and *bring him in*. We ask the fortunate so to alter or moderate their claims as to make them consistent with those of the unfortunate" (p. 672). Perry claims that a "hypothetical application" (p. 659) of the principle of inclusiveness makes it

> evident that a situation in which both the one and the millions were happy *would be* better. We do not attempt to compare the weight of the majority and minority interests with one another, or balance one man's loss against a million's gain. We acknowledge that there are amounts or degrees of value associated with each party, between which it is impossible to discriminate because they are incommensurable. [But w]e fall back on the principle that just as the fulfilment of an interest is better than its defeat, whatever the intensity or grade of the interest, so a situation which fulfils that interest will, other things being equal, be better than a situation which defeats it. (p. 674)

That is, were it possible both to have the millions happy and to alleviate the torture of the lost soul, that would be better. Perry's suggestion, quoted above, is to achieve this by "ask[ing] the fortunate so to alter or moderate their claims as to make them consistent with those of the unfortunate." But is a "moderated" interest really the same interest?[2] Only if the desires of the fortunate are the same

---

2. Perry might seem to equate all interests with what I call underlying desires. A desire is underlying to the extent that it survives isolation tests—that is, to the extent that the subject would still have and act on that desire even if its satisfaction were not a means to the satisfaction of some further desire. When Perry describes the way "the fortunate" could "alter or moderate their claims" for the sake of James's lost soul—and, in general, how individuals can alter their desires so as to render them harmonious with their fellows'

before and after "bringing in" the lost soul can the desires satisfied in the latter case be related to those satisfied in the former case as set and proper subset.

General Theory of Value contains a lengthy and complicated discussion of the ways interests can be "integrated" to each other. Perry says, for example, that we can understand how the behavior of an individual will be different when he has two interests rather than either in isolation, without having to say that the interests are themselves altered by existing in combination.

> A resultant of forces exhibits the same type of structure. The body does not move in accordance with the nature of either the centrifugal or the centripetal force in isolation, but does move strictly in accordance with the nature of both forces operating jointly. Its motion can be produced wholly by the application of the two forces in question without the application of any additional force, and its behavior can be resolved into them without any residuum. Although the component forces may not be recognizable in their joint operation, their presence and persistence is revealed by the fact that when the centripetal force is removed the body moves centrifugally and vice versa. (1926, p. 661)

In some cases, it is not implausible to say that two interests in combination are wholly satisfied through behavior that would not be said wholly to satisfy either taken in isolation. For example, Perry describes "a man who loves both sport and business" as fully satisfying both interests "through his thinking out and adoption of a plan" (p. 660). If the individual had only one interest, in golf or in business, then action according to a plan of reserving golf and business to certain times of the week would not fully satisfy the interest in question. Yet when the individual has two underlying interests, in golf and in business, it does not seem implausible to say that each is fully satisfied by the plan in question.

However, in James's lost soul case, it would be highly implausible to say that the "moderation" Perry requests of "the fortunate" does not involve them abandoning certain desires and forming others. The desire to have 1/1,000,000 of the food at the table is different from the desire to have 1/1,000,001 of the food. Realistically, of course, the choice in James's example is much more stark. The "alteration" Perry is asking "the fortunate" to make is to give up their desires for utopian satisfactions and to accept something like the status quo. But the desires for utopia and for the status quo cannot plausibly be said to be the same

---

desires—he writes as if the interests in question remain the same because the underlying desires remain the same as they "moderate their claims." But, on a view like mine or Perry's, the satisfaction of any desire is (at least considered in and of itself) a good thing. Perry defines value as "the object of any interest" and he unpacks interest in terms of desire. On such a view, any satisfaction of a desire must create some value. My desire to open the door may be a paradigm example of a desire that is not underlying (I open the door only in order to accomplish other things), but it is a desire nevertheless, and its satisfaction would be a good thing.

desire. Perry is correct to characterize the application of the principle of inclusiveness in this case as "hypothetical," precisely because the situation is structured so that it is impossible to satisfy everyone's desires. Substantial alterations in the desires of "the fortunate" are necessary to set the stage for harmonious satisfaction of everyone's desires. So Perry implicitly abandons his own restriction on the applicability of the principle of inclusiveness (that the interests compared be related as set and proper subset) during his treatment of James's lost soul example.

Although I agree that the principle is more broadly applicable than Perry explicitly admits, as a utilitarian at heart, I cannot agree with him that the intuitively correct solution of the lost soul case is obviously to "bring in" the lost soul. Perry expresses "the firm conviction that the happiness of a million somehow fails utterly to compensate or even to mitigate the torture of one" (1926, p. 671). If the choice were between something just short of utopia for all versus utopia for a million and hell for one, I might agree. But if the choice were between the status quo and utopia for all save one, I would be hard pressed to accept the status quo. This is a classic "test case" for utilitarianism, in response to which a committed utilitarian has two options: (1) bite the bullet and accept the putatively unjust torture of the lost soul while pointing out that such dramatic choices are not met with in real life or (2) push for details that will imply that, even in utilitarian terms, the utopia may not be so grand ("Is the 'lost soul' literally being tortured? If so, by whom? Do the million know that their happiness is being bought at his expense? If so, what effects does this have on their humanity?" and so on).

A better example to use in defending broadened applicability of the principle of inclusiveness is Jack's desire to break the record for serial murder. Here the utilitarian is convinced that the best thing to do is doom Jack's desire, and presumably Perry would agree. I agree with Perry that the application of the principle of inclusiveness is limited, but not in the extremely narrow way he believes, and in particular I think it can be used to shed light on this type of case.

The Priority of Ground Projects (Principle P2')

The satisfaction (and dissatisfaction) of interests is a very nuanced affair, and as a result I do not think that Perry's principle of inclusiveness can be used to shed light on every situation or even on most of them. Only where (1) the interests involved are of certain specified types and (2) there is a clear-cut trade off between dooming one interest and ensuring the satisfaction of another—only in such cases is the principle likely to be helpful. Nevertheless, I argue, the principle can be used to generalize from the cases in which it is applicable to the general presumptions expressed in P1 and P2'. In this section, I argue for principle P2', beginning from Jack's desire to break the record for serial murder (which Donald

Harvey recently raised to thirty-seven from John Wayne Gacy's record of thirty-three).

Jack's desire is like the desire to succeed in a certain profession, or to live a certain kind of life, and each of the persons Jack desires to kill has, among his or her desires, a similar desire to live a certain kind of life. Suppose, for example, that among Jack's intended victims is Jill, an aspiring academic. Jack and Jill both have what Bernard Williams calls a ground project, "a nexus of projects . . . which are closely related to [one's] existence and which to a significant degree give a meaning to [one's] life" (1981, pp. 13, 12). Elsewhere Williams defines a categorical desire as one that answers the question "Why is life worth living?" (1973, pp. 85–86). So one's ground project is a nexus of categorical desires. For some people, this nexus may be very simple: Jack, for instance, may have only one categorical desire—to break the record for serial murder. For others, like Jill, the nexus may be complex and contain many things making life worth living: the desire to achieve national prominence in her field, coupled with the desires to raise a family, to participate in community government, and so on.

Now compare these ground projects to a noncategorical desire, such as my present desire to have coffee to drink first thing tomorrow morning. This is not a ground project, because I will not cease to think life worth living if this desire goes unsatisfied, and it is not a categorical desire because the pursuit of its satisfaction does not suffice to make life worth living for me. To be sure, the satisfaction of such a simple desire can require the satisfaction of several others. If I have used the last of the coffee this morning, I will have to go to the store and get more before tomorrow, and that can involve forming and satisfying a number of desires (to find my wallet, to get my bicycle out of the garage, to lock it up before entering the store, and so on). So the satisfaction of a noncategorical desire can involve the satisfaction of numerous other desires. But the satisfaction of a ground project normally involves far more than this. A ground project is an especially inclusive desire in the sense that its satisfaction normally requires the satisfaction, across a lengthy period of time, of innumerable noncategorical desires.

In the serial murder case, we are intuitively certain that it would be worse to satisfy Jack's ground project than it would be to satisfy those of Jill and his other victims. In expressing this judgment, we are likely to appeal to the principle of utility—we are likely to say that we know that the satisfaction of Jack's ground project would be worse than the satisfaction of his victims' ground projects, because more disutility would be created in the former case. But we really do not have any way of assigning cardinal utilities to the satisfaction of various desires, including ground projects. Nevertheless, I submit that we are certain that the principle of utility would imply our intuitive judgment, because we are certain that the satisfaction or dissatisfaction of similar kinds of interests creates similar amounts of cardinal utility or disutility. Even though we do not know how much cardinal utility the satisfaction of a ground project creates, we are confident that it creates more than the satisfaction of my desire to have coffee tomorrow morning, and we are confident about this because the desires are so different in kind.

Ground projects define desires that are distinctive in kind, because their satisfaction requires the satisfaction across time (usually a lifetime or a significant portion thereof) of innumerable noncategorical desires. Many of these noncategorical desires in turn require the satisfaction of other noncategorical desires, but on nothing like the scale of a normal ground project. There is, therefore, a hierarchical relationship between one's ground project and all of one's other desires. Satisfaction of (or even productive prosecution of) one's ground project requires the satisfaction across a lengthy period of time (usually a lifetime or a significant portion thereof) of innumerable noncategorical desires. But not vice versa. Assuming that satisfaction of interests from similar locations in different peoples' hierarchies creates similar amounts of value, the principle of inclusiveness is applicable to the serial killer case, and so we can confidently conclude that it would be better to doom Jack's ground project and satisfy the ground projects of his many victims rather than vice versa. This is because, normally or in general, the satisfaction of various ground projects creates comparable amounts of value and the dooming of various ground projects creates comparable amounts of disvalue. Therefore, dooming one ground project (Jack's) would be better than dooming many (his victims').

The assumption at work in the foregoing treatment of the serial killer case can be formalized as:

> (A3) Generally speaking, ensuring the satisfaction of interests from similar levels in similar hierarchies of different individuals creates similar amounts of value, and the dooming of interests from similar levels in similar hierarchies of different individuals creates similar levels of disvalue.

When coupled with the foregoing observations about the hierarchical relationship between ground projects and noncategorical desires, (A3) yields principle P2':

> (P2') Generally speaking, the satisfaction of ground projects is more important than the satisfaction of noncategorical desires.

Two things must be emphasized about this principle.

First, P2' expresses a presumptive and rebuttable generalization about the comparative value of ground projects vis-à-vis noncategorical desires. It is, at least in principle, possible to have as one's ground project a desire that can be finally satisfied within a short period of time and without satisfying many other desires. But this would be an unusual ground project. Normally, ground projects cannot be finally satisfied in a short period of time; normally, the prosecution of a ground project requires the ongoing formation and satisfaction of innumerable desires across a period of time on the order of a normal life span. Notice that, although Jack's ground project could be finally satisfied in relatively short order (Gacy took six years to kill thirty-three men and boys, but perhaps Jack could squeeze thirty-eight murders into a month), his forming this ground project requires that he live long enough to form a ground project at all, and this requires the formation and satisfaction of innumerable desires across a period of years. By contrast, the satisfaction of my desire to have coffee tomorrow morning requires only that I make it through the night.[3]

Second, and more significant, P2' is a generalization about the comparative value of interests of two types taken in isolation rather than a generalization about states of affairs. Therefore, conclusions reached using it are not statements about obligations (or even permissions). To say that the satisfaction of interest A would create more value than the satisfaction of either B or C is not equivalent to saying that A ought to be satisfied rather than B and C. For it could be that the value created by the satisfaction of B and C, taken together, is greater than that created by the satisfaction of A. For example, if the cardinal utilities of the satisfaction of these interests were $A = 5$, $B = 3$, and $C = 3$, then the satisfaction of B and C would be better than the satisfaction of A by itself. However, the problem of assigning cardinal utilities to the various interests in two states of affairs means that all we can do with any degree of confidence and precision is to compare the value created by the satisfaction or dissatisfaction of a desire from one category to that created by the satisfaction or dissatisfaction of a desire from another category. In this respect, P2' behaves more like a rights principle than the principle of utility. That is, rights-based principles typically compare rights pairwise: A takes precedence over B and A takes precedence over C, so A takes precedence, irrespective of the aggregate utility of $B + C$. Similarly, principle P2' compares desires pairwise: A (a ground project) is more important than B (a noncategorical desire) and A is more important than C (another noncategorical desire), so A is most important, irrespective of the aggregate utility of satisfying B and C together. Nevertheless, P2' is a generalization justified by the principle of utility in conjunction with assumption A3, and so it is utilitarian in spirit and in its foundation. In light of the problem of assigning cardinal utilities to various interests, we are left with only principles of this sort; we cannot compare the cardinal utility of a ground project's satisfaction to that of many noncategorical desires taken in the aggregate. Therefore we cannot conclude from an application of P2' that one course of action is obligatory or even that it is permissible. Conclusions reached using principle P2' cannot be stated in the deontic modalities of permission and

3. Red Watson points out to me that "you had to learn to like coffee and become addicted to caffeine, earn the money to buy it, etc." This is true. But again, the prosecution of a ground project normally occurs across a longer period of time than even that required to learn things requisite to forming a desire like my (sadly, addiction-based) desire for coffee.

obligation (i.e., not in terms of right and wrong). All that an application of P2' justifies us in saying is that the satisfaction of one interest probably would create more utility than the satisfaction of another, because they are of two different kinds, and this is generally true of two instances of these kinds. Nevertheless, this gives us a prima facie reason for satisfying a ground project rather than a non-categorical desire, when the two come into conflict, and a prima facie case for satisfying more ground projects rather than fewer.

Principle P2' implies neither that it is obligatory nor that it is permissible to kill rats whose behavior threatens human ground projects, but, in light of the problem with assigning comparative magnitudes to the satisfaction of the various interests involved, P2' provides us with as good a reason as we can hope to have for doing so. This addresses VanDeVeer's worry once we acknowledge that, with very few likely exceptions, only human beings have ground projects. Dogs and cats, for example, almost certainly have desires that transcend the present. When a lion flushes a wildebeest in the direction of a hidden pridemate (anecdote reported in Griffin 1992, pp. 64–65), or (more prosaical) when my cat comes from the back room to where I am sitting and, having gotten my attention by jumping in my lap, leads me to the back door to be let out, she undoubtedly has a desire for something in the future. But cats and dogs are concerned about a very near future. The desire to catch a prey animal here now, or the desire to get a human being from the other room to come open the door to the outside, is not on a par with aspiring to longer life or to a way of life. We do not observe nonhuman mammals providing for their distant future in an organized way except where (as with a squirrel saving acorns or a bird building a nest) the behavior is more plausibly attributed to instinct than desire. Formulating and prosecuting a ground project requires a level of conceptual sophistication that almost no nonhuman animal has. Perhaps some of the great apes (gorillas, chimpanzees, and orangutans) or some cetaceans have ground projects, but none of the animals the average person comes into contact with on a regular basis would appear to. (Many Africans came into regular contact with great apes before their ranges became extremely restricted, but almost no one does today.) Embracing P2', then, alleviates VanDeVeer's worry: we have a prima facie reason to believe that killing animals whose behavior actually threatens the ground projects of human beings is better than allowing those ground projects to be threatened.

However, it bears emphasizing that not just anything goes where human use of animals is concerned. Just as the principle of inclusiveness gives us a reason for satisfying the ground projects of Jack's intended victims rather that satisfying his ground project, it gives us a reason for preferring ground projects with minimal negative impacts on the interests of others, whatever those interests are (ground projects, categorical desires, or biological interests) and whether they are the interests of humans or nonhumans. Because the satisfaction of interests is always a good thing, adopting a ground project that does not doom the interests of others is better than adopting a ground project that does necessarily doom the interests of others. This, after all, is why Jill's ground project is morally better than Jack's—its satisfaction does not doom anyone else's ground project. But, by the same token, a ground project that does not require for its satisfaction the dooming of various interests of nonhuman animals or plants is thus a far better ground project than one that does require their dooming. This is emphasized in the following principle:

> (P3) Other things being equal, it is better to satisfy ground projects that require, as a condition of their satisfaction, the dooming of fewer interests of others.

We can call this the principle of least necessary harm (acknowledging that, unanalyzed, the notion of necessity is of very little help [Finsen 1990]).

It is also important to emphasize here that P2' is not a speciesist principle as is P2 and that the retreat from P2 to P2' is not ad hoc. Principle P2 gives preference to human interests as such, (i.e., because they are human interests). Principle P2' gives preference to ground projects not because almost no nonhuman animals have ground projects, but because whatever the species membership of an individual with a ground project, that ground project normally stands in a hierarchical relationship to that individual's noncategorical desires, and this, in light of assumption A3 gives us a prima facie but a good reason for believing that satisfaction of that ground project is more important than the satisfaction of any noncategorical desire of that or any other individual. It is a matter of contingent fact that no (or almost no) nonhuman animals have ground projects. It is also a matter of contingent fact that some human beings have no ground projects (most obviously the irreversibly comotose but also some extremely mentally retarded or brain-injured individuals). So principle P2' is not a speciesist principle. Notice, also, that the principle of inclusiveness gives us no reason for embracing principle P2; the principle of inclusiveness gives us no reason to believe that the satisfaction of a desire will create more value simply because it is a human's. So the principle of inclusiveness gives us no reason for embracing P2 but it does give us a reason for embracing the weaker P2'.

PRIORITY OF DESIRES (PRINCIPLE P1)

Principle P2' alleviates Passmore's worry, since it implies that it is better to eat nonhuman organisms and thereby doom all of their interests than to doom one's ground project. But the principle of inclusiveness and assumption A3 can also be used to defend principle P1, which implies more specifically that (other things being equal) it is better to eat plants than it is to eat animals (or at least animals with desires).

The satisfaction of a particular noncategorical desire does not necessarily supervene upon the satisfaction of myriad biological interests of the organism in the same way that the satisfaction of a particular ground project normally supervenes upon the satisfaction of myriad noncategorical interests. Nevertheless, the general capacity to form and satisfy desires (even noncategorical ones) depends on the ongoing satisfaction of the lion's share of the individual's biological interests. This is analogous to the hierarchical relationship that normally obtains between one's ground project and one's noncategorical desires. A human being, another mammal, a bird, or an octopus cannot continue to form and satisfy desires unless a large share of its biological interests receive ongoing satisfaction. An individual's capacity to form and satisfy desires thus supervenes upon the ongoing satisfaction of myriad biological interests of that individual. Myriad, but certainly not all. For although I have a biological interest in my vasa deferentia continuing to pass sperm, I can continue to form and satisfy desires after having them tied off. Still, I could not continue to form and satisfy desires without adequate nutrition, without my gastrointestinal tract, my heart and lungs, my limbic system, and so on all continuing to function. Nor could any nonhuman animal such as a mammal or a bird continue to form and satisfy desires without the satisfaction of analogous biological interests.

Thus the general capacity for desire supervenes upon the ongoing satisfaction of myriad interests of the only kind that desireless creatures have, namely biological interests. Hence we can say that, in general, the life of an animal that has desires creates more value than the life of an organism that does not. For, although both require the satisfaction of myriad biological interests, the life of a desiring creature requires this plus the satisfaction of myriad other interests: an admittedly indeterminate number of its desires. We thus arrive at principle P1:

(P1) Generally speaking, the death of an entity that had desires is a worse thing than the death of an entity that does not.

Here again, two things must be emphasized.

First, just as with P2', we cannot conclude from an application of P1 that one course of action is obligatory or even that it is permissible. All that an application of P1 justifies us in saying is that the loss of an organism with desires probably would create more disutility than the loss from the world of an organism without desires. Nevertheless, this gives us a prima facie reason for lacto-ovo vegetarianism, or at least pescovegetarianism. (A lacto-ovo vegetarian eats by-products such as milk and eggs that can be obtained from animals without slaughtering them. A pescovegetarian eats fish but no red meat or fowl.)

Second, P1 is not a license to do just anything with desireless creatures. Just as the principle of inclusiveness gives us a reason for thinking that those ground projects are better that doom fewer interests of others, it also gives us a reason for thinking that desires that doom fewer biological interests of others are better than those that doom more. If we have reason to believe that two noncategorical desires are similarly situated hierarchically among an individual's noncategorical desires, then we have reason to say that it would be better to satisfy the desire that dooms fewer biological interests of others. The "if" clause is necessary, because not all noncategorical desires are on a par. Some require for their satisfaction the satisfaction of numerous other desires, while some do not. Only if we have reason to believe that two desires are similarly situated hierarchically can we be confident that the satisfaction of the desire that does not doom some biological interests would be better than the satisfaction of the desire that does.

Consider, for example, the desire to torch the forest, "to see how all would burn." This desire could be related to the individual's other desires in various ways. It might be a way of fulfilling a Cristoesque ground project of executing a grand and dramatic kind of performance art in nature. On the other hand, it might be an idle wish for a moment's entertainment. This is in fact how Mary Midgley represents the desire in her 1983 paper. In the former case, if it is possible to fulfill the individual's ground project in a way that involves the deaths of fewer plants, then P3 implies that this would be better. In the latter case, P3 does not apply. However, there certainly are other ways of amusing oneself for a moment that need not involve the destruction of thousands of plants. That is, Midgley's Robinson Crusoe could certainly form other desires that would be similarly situated in his hierarchy of interests, the satisfaction of which would not doom the biological interests of thousands of plants.

The principle of least necessary harm should be amended to reflect this consideration:

(P3') Other things being equal, of two desires similarly situated in an individual's hierarchy of interests, it is better to satisfy the desire that requires as a condition of its satisfaction the dooming of fewer interests of others (whether these interests be defined by desires or biological interests).

This revised version of P3 preserves the original insight—that all ground projects are similarly situated vis-à-vis all noncategorical desires—and couples it with the insight that, of two noncategorical desires similarly situated in an individual's hierarchy of interests, the satisfaction of the desire that dooms fewer biological interests is preferable.

A Hierarchy of Interests

The extended application of Perry's principle of inclusiveness that I have defended in this chapter leads to a rough hierarchy of interests as expressed in principles P1 and P2': ground projects are generally more important than noncategorical desires, and desires are generally more important than biological interests. This implies a rough hierarchy of life forms: human beings are generally more important than other animals that have desires such as birds and at least most nonhuman mammals, and these are in turn more important than organisms without desires, such as insects, plants, and microorganisms.

Hierarchies of this sort are currently frowned upon in some quarters, but as Passmore's and VanDeVeer's worries suggest, any workable ethics will contain some hierarchies of this sort. Albert Schweitzer is renowned for assiduously refusing to prioritize forms of life and their various interests. In his *Philosophy of Civilization*, he maintains that

> Whenever I in any way sacrifice or injure life, I am not within the sphere of the ethical, but I become guilty, whether it be egoistically guilty for the sake of maintaining my own existence or welfare, or unegoistically guilty for the sake of maintaining a greater number of other existences or their welfare. (1955, p. 325)

Here Schweitzer clearly says that even killing for self-preservation incurs guilt. Yet he also admits that the "necessity to destroy and to injure life is imposed upon me" at every step (p. 316), which implies that we cannot help but incur guilt all the time. Elsewhere he appears to contradict himself, saying that "Whenever I injure life of any sort, I must be quite clear whether it is necessary. Beyond the unavoidable, I must never go" (p. 318), which suggests that "unavoidable" or "necessary" injuries are permissible. It may be that Schweitzer's point is one with which I agree, namely that any adverse impact on the interests of any organism (even a disease microbe) introduces some evil into the world. If this were the meaning of the former passage, then it would be consistent with the latter passage, because (as any utilitarian will admit) the production of some evil can be justified by the preservation or production of good. Speaking in terms of unavoidable guilt is a confusing way of making this point, however. Probably Schweitzer's overarching aim is to urge people, in very dramatic terms, to take seriously decisions involving injury or death to living things of any species. With that laudable goal I agree. But Schweitzer's own talk about the necessity of injury and death gives the lie to any practically useful ethics entirely free of hierarchies. Any workable ethics must involve some hierarchy of interests, and, if only some forms of life have the favored kinds of interests, a hierarchy of life forms follows.

Basic Interests

I conclude this chapter with a brief response to the allegation that principle P1 elevates even trivial desires (such as Maude's desire to smoke) above putatively more important biological interests (such as Maude's interest in the continued functioning of her lungs). First I must introduce the concept of a basic interest. Henry Shue defines a basic *right* as one that is "essential to the enjoyment of all other rights": "When a right is genuinely basic, any attempt to enjoy any other right by sacrificing the basic right would be quite literally self-defeating, cutting the ground from beneath itself" (1980, p. 19). Analogously, a basic interest is one that in the normal course of events must be satisfied if any other interests of the same individual are to be satisfied. It is not that the satisfaction of such an interest ensures the satisfaction of other interests but rather that the satisfaction of any other interest requires the satisfaction of this interest. Its satisfaction is a necessary but not a sufficient condition for other interests' satisfaction, and this is why (to paraphrase Shue) any attempt to satisfy other interests by sacrificing the basic interest would be quite literally self-defeating, by cutting the ground from beneath itself.

Probably all interests that are basic in this sense are biological interests. Not all biological interests are basic (my interest in continued functioning of my vasa deferentia, for instance), but many are, including Maude's interest in the continued functioning of her lungs. In the normal course of events, the ongoing satisfaction of this interest is a necessary condition for the satisfaction of every other interest an individual may have, both biological interests and desires (both categorical and noncategorical). There are, of course, exceptions. The final satisfaction of a categorical desire for martyrdom could require the defeat of one's general interest in cardiovascular health. But notice that the satisfaction of even such a self-destructive desire would (like Jack's serial murder ground project) require, up until the bitter end, the ongoing satisfaction of basic interests like that in cardiovascular health.

Nevertheless, basic interests are not categorical. All of one's basic interests could be satisfied without one having, in any meaningful way, a life worth living. The objection that P1 elevates trivial desires above important biological interests plays upon the putative importance of basic interests. Basic interests are indeed important, but not because their satisfaction considered in and of itself produces so much value. A life in which only one's most basic interests were satisfied would be only marginally worth living. Basic interests are important because their satisfaction is a necessary (but not a sufficient) condition for the satisfaction of the most inclusive desires—our ground projects. Our ground projects are built on the bedrock of our basic interests, and the life of a normal human being is more valuable than the life of almost any nonhuman organism precisely because almost no other kind of organism has ground projects.

CHAPTER FIVE

Can Animal Rights Activists
Be Environmentalists?

MY OWN VIEW is not, strictly speaking, an animal rights philosophy. My view does not restrict moral standing to sentient organisms, nor do I employ the concept of moral obligation, let alone that of moral rights. Nevertheless, my view resembles animal rights views insofar as I find preeminent value in the lives of individual sentient organisms, and this places it in dubious company, since most environmental philosophers believe that animal rights views are incompatible with sound environmental policy.

Notoriously, it was J. Baird Callicott who, in his early paper "Animal Liberation: A Triangular Affair," appeared to delight in driving a very deep wedge between environmentalism and animal rights. To appreciate how hegemonic this view of the animal rights–environmental ethics split has become among environmental ethicists, consider the following quotations. Under a title extending Callicott's amorous metaphor ("Animal Liberation and Environmental Ethics: Bad Marriage, Quick Divorce"), Mark Sagoff wrote:

> Environmentalists cannot be animal liberationists. Animal liberationists cannot be environmentalists. . . . Moral obligations to nature cannot be enlightened or explained—one cannot even take the first step—by appealing to the rights of animals. (1984, pp. 304, 306)

Eric Katz relies on the now familiar dichotomy in advising businesses engaged in animal research about how to blunt the criticisms of animal rights activists:

> I suggest that the adoption by business of a more conscious environmentalism can serve as a defense against the animal liberation movement. This strategy may seem paradoxical: how can business defend its use of animals by advocating the protection of the environment? But the paradox disappears once we see that animal liberation and environmentalism are incompatible practical moral doctrines. (1990, p. 224)

Although Callicott subsequently regretted the fulminatory rhetoric of his "Triangular Affair" piece (see Callicott 1989), he continues to think of animal rights and environmental ethics as incompatible. For example, he argues for moral monism on the grounds that a pluralism embracing both animal rights and environmental ethics would be inconsistent, because "animal rights would prohibit controlling the populations of sentient animals by means of hunting, while environmental ethics would permit it" (1994, p. 52). Even Bryan Norton, whose overarching concern in *Toward Unity among Environmentalists* is to find points of agreement at the level of practice amid disagreement at the level of moral principle, writes as if animal rights and environmental ethics can never be reconciled. During a discussion of deep ecologists' profession of biocentric egalitarianism—the view that all organisms are equal (ostensibly very similar to animal rights theorists' claim of animal [or at least vertebrate] equality)—Norton states that

> As academics, spokespersons for deep ecology have been able to avoid adopting policies on difficult, real-world cases such as elk destroying their wolf-free ranges, feral goats destroying indigenous vegetation on fragile lands, or park facilities overwhelmed by human visitors. (1991, p. 222)

Norton goes on to explain that equal rights for nonhuman animals is environmentally unsound because "It can never be 'fair' by human standards to kill 10 percent of an elk population because it exceeds the capacity of its range" (p. 223). That even a consensus-seeking pragmatist such as Norton writes as if animal rights views are systematically environmentally unsound suggests just how deeply rooted is the perceived dichotomy between environmental ethics and animal rights.

Self-professed animal rights activists have, I think, contributed to the perception that animal rights views have environmentally unsound implications by truncating and radicalizing their views. Animal rights activists have very little interest in or need for being clear about what their philosophical views are and what those views do and do not imply. In political debates, it is often impossible to describe one's position fully and is often ineffective to do so even if one has time. "Animals are not ours to eat, wear, or experiment on" is a politically expedient slogan for someone who believes that radical reform is called for, even if that person actually believes that some uses are acceptable under some conditions. The necessity of producing sound-bite-sized quotations for the news media contributes to the truncation of peoples' position statements, but also a general principle of negotiation is to begin by demanding more than one is ultimately willing to settle for. So animal rights activists have good reasons for their commonly espoused impatience with philosophical subtlety. But there is a difference between a philosophy and a bumper sticker, and, once we move beyond political posturing and sloganeering to a careful examination of the philosophical bases of the animal rights movement, we see that convergence is possible at the level of policy between animal rights views and the views of environmentalists.[1]

Most of this chapter is devoted to a detailed, critical examination of the hunting issue from the perspectives of the dominant animal rights philosophies: Peter Singer's utilitarianism and Tom Regan's rights view. My goal is to show that, in general, views such as Singer's, Regan's, and mine, in which preeminent value is ascribed to the lives of individual sentient creatures, can support hunting in every situation in which an environmentalist feels compelled to support it. I leave the implications of my own view for environmental policy in the background until the following chapter. I conclude the present chapter with brief remarks on predation in general and on the place of predation in human nature in particular.

THERAPEUTIC HUNTING OF OBLIGATORY MANAGEMENT SPECIES

As I understand it, the antagonism of environmental philosophers toward animal rights views grows out of their perception that the practical implications of animal rights views are antienvironmental in two basic ways.

1. With regard to wildlife population control, the concerns are that
   a. hunting would be prohibited, even when it is required to preserve the health or integrity of an ecosystem, and
   b. humans would have an obligation to prevent natural predation (including not restoring locally extinct predators).
2. With regard to preserving biodiversity, the concerns are that
   a. it would be impermissible to remove or kill destructive exotics, and
   b. it would be impermissible to breed members of endangered species in captivity.

In this chapter, I concentrate on hunting and predation. What I would have to say about biodiversity from the animals' perspective directly parallels what I have to say about it from the axiologically anthropocentric perspective adopted in the following chapter.

When teaching the hunting issue, I find it useful to distinguish among three types of hunting in terms of the purposes hunting is taken to serve. By "therapeutic hunting," I mean hunting motivated by and designed to secure the aggregate welfare of the target species, the integrity of its ecosystem, or both. By "subsistence hunting," I mean hunting aimed at securing food for human beings.

---

1. Norton (1991) emphasizes the distinction between consensus (agreement at the level of policy based on agreement at the level of moral theory) and convergence (agreement at the level of policy despite disagreement at the level of moral theory).

By "sport hunting," I mean hunting aimed at maintaining religious or cultural traditions, at reenacting national or evolutionary history, at practicing certain skills, or just at securing a trophy. Many would prefer to recognize a distinction within this third category between hunting for sport and hunting as a ritual. Although there may be some important differences, I class them together, because both activities serve human needs (which is what distinguishes both sport and subsistence hunting from therapeutic hunting), though needs that are less fundamental (in the sense of universal) than nutrition (which is what distinguishes subsistence hunting from both ritual and sport hunting).

Obviously these are abstract archetypes. Wildlife managers designing a hunt and hunters going into the field almost always have some composite of these three goals in mind. Inuits taking a whale are engaged in subsistence hunting, but so is a Hill Country Texan who likes venison. And both are engaged in sport hunting as I conceive of it: the Inuits' communal life is structured around hunting—it has great social and religious significance—but so is the Texan's insofar as he views hunting as an expression of his cultural or evolutionary history.

This typology based on the ends hunting is supposed to serve helps us to say where the prospects for convergence lie. Significantly, the defenses that hunters and environmentalists most often offer in the face of criticism by animal rights activists—that it is necessary to prevent overpopulation and environmental degradation—clearly are defenses of therapeutic hunting specifically, not of sport or subsistence hunting. The thesis I defend here is that environmentalists and animal rights activists can agree on the moral necessity of therapeutic hunting of obligatory management species.

I owe the term "obligatory management species" to Ron Howard of the Texas Agricultural Extension Service, who distinguishes between "obligatory" and "permissive" management species in the following way. An obligatory management species is one that has a fairly regular tendency to overshoot the carrying capacity of its range, to the detriment of its own future generations and those of other species. A permissive management species is one that does not normally exhibit this tendency. Examples of obligatory management species are ungulates (hooved mammals such as white-tailed and mule deer, elk, and bison) and elephants. Examples of permissive management species are mourning doves, cottontail rabbits, gray squirrels, bobwhite, and blue quail.[2] It is not that permissive management species do not become overpopulated. They do every year, in the straightforward sense of producing more young than their habitat can feed through the winter. But they usually do not degrade their habitat in ways that threaten future generations of their own or other species. This is what makes

2. These are Ron Howard's examples in personal communication dated 18 June 1992. Obviously, in which category a species belongs can change—for example, when rabbits were introduced to Australia, they became obligatory management species.

their management environmentally optional, or "merely permissible" in Ron Howard's terminology. By contrast, management of ungulates (and some other species) is environmentally necessary, or "obligatory" in Howard's terms.[3]

Environmental groups have taken great pains in recent years to distance themselves from animal rights groups, because they fear that the widespread perception of animal rights activists as antiscientific romantics will rub off on them. Much of the distancing has had to do with the hunting issue. *Audubon* magazine announced an article with the scathing title "Fuzzy Wuzzy Thinking about Animal Rights" (Conniff 1990) with the cover teaser "Animal Rights: Ignorance about Nature." The Wisconsin Greens adopted a resolution condemning Madison's Alliance for Animals for disrupting hunts in Blue Mound State Park (Julie Smith 1991). And a Sierra Club fundraiser said in a phone conversation that the club was not "doing more to expose the enormous environmental damage caused by factory farming because they wanted to keep their membership as large as possible" (Bean 1991).

Still, environmentalists do not uniformly support hunting. Audubon and the Sierra Club both oppose hunting in the national parks, and the Texas chapters of both clubs recently opposed a bill that opened the state's parks to recreational hunting. Texas law already allowed hunting in state parks on an ad hoc basis, "as sound biological management practices warrant" (Texas State Code, Title 5 [Hunting and Fishing], §62.062[a])—for example, to deal with ungulate population irruptions. But S.B. 179, which was signed into law 18 May 1993, amended the state's Parks and Recreation Code to allow classification of state parks as "game management areas" as well as "recreational areas, natural areas, or historical areas" (S.B. 179, Section 1; Texas Code, Title 2 [Parks and Recreational Areas], §13.001[b]). According to its *State Capitol Report*, the "Sierra Club opposes any bill that will shift the burden of proof from no hunting in state parks unless 'biologically necessary', to hunting is allowed unless proven harmful to the area's resources" (Sierra Club, Lone Star Chapter, 1993). That is not particularly well stated, but the sense is clear enough: the Sierra Club opposes allowing sport hunting on a regular basis in state parks, but it will support sport hunting in the state parks on an ad hoc basis, when "biologically necessary."

Sierra's and Audubon's position on hunting in national and state parks illustrates how the only hunting environmentalists feel compelled to support is "biologically necessary" hunting—that is, therapeutic hunting—and therapeutic hunting normally is necessary only where obligatory management species are

---

3. It might be preferable to speak in terms of "necessary" and "optional" rather than "obligatory" and "permissible," because Howard's labels are intended to be descriptive rather than normative. Also, note the qualification, in the penultimate section of this chapter, that, even among obligatory management species, hunting is not always necessary to prevent environmental damage.

concerned. Officially, both organizations are noncommittal on sport hunting outside of the national and Texas state parks. This mirrors a difference of opinion within the environmental community. Many environmentalists would prefer that sport hunting that is not also therapeutic be stopped, and many would prefer that natural predators be restored to levels at which human hunting is less often biologically necessary. But many environmentalists are also avid hunters who attach great ritual significance to their hunting.

So the only hunting that environmentalists feel compelled to support is therapeutic hunting of obligatory management species. However, the received interpretation of the animal rights–environmental ethics split is that animal rights activists must oppose hunting even when it is biologically necessary. Yet when we look behind the sound-bite-sized quotations and political slogans of self-professed animal rights activists to examine carefully formulated animal rights philosophies, we see that it is not necessary for animal rightists to oppose environmentally sound hunting. Animal rightists can support exactly the same policy in regard to hunting that environmental groups like Audubon and the Sierra Club support in regard to the national and state parks. The easiest way to bring this out is by making the now familiar and basic philosophical distinction between an animal liberation or animal welfare view and a true animal rights view and by beginning with the former's application to the hunting question.

ANIMAL LIBERATION AND THERAPEUTIC HUNTING

Peter Singer's 1975 book *Animal Liberation* has become the Bible of the animal rights movement. Singer wrote that book for popular consumption, and in it he speaks loosely of animals having "moral rights." But all that he means by this is that animals (or at least "higher animals," such as vertebrates) have some basic moral standing and that there are right and wrong ways of treating them. In later, more philosophically rigorous work (summarized in his *Practical Ethics*), he explicitly eschews the term "rights" by noting that, as a utilitarian ethical theorist, he not only denies that animals have moral rights but states that in his view neither do human beings. Singer wrote *Animal Liberation* in the vernacular to make his arguments appeal to the widest variety of audiences—he did not want to tie his criticisms of agriculture and animal research to his specific moral philosophy.

When ethicists speak of an individual "having moral rights," they mean something much more specific than that the individual has some basic moral standing and that there are right and wrong ways of treating him or her (or it). Although there is much controversy as to the specifics, there is general agreement on this: to attribute moral rights to an individual is to assert that the individual has some kind of special moral dignity—that is, there are certain things that cannot justifiably be done to him or her (or it) for the sake of benefit to others.

For this reason, moral rights have been characterized as "trump cards" against utilitarian arguments. Utilitarian arguments are based on aggregate benefits and aggregate harms. Utilitarianism is usually defined as the view that right actions maximize aggregate happiness. In principle, nothing is inherently or intrinsically wrong, according to a utilitarian; any action could be justified under some possible circumstances. One way of characterizing rights views in ethics, by contrast, is that some things, regardless of the consequences, are simply wrong to do to individuals and that moral rights single out these things.

Although a technical and stipulative definition of the term, this philosophical usage reflects a familiar concept. One familiar way appeals to the rights of individuals are used in day-to-day discussions is to assert, in effect, that there is a limit to what individuals can be forced to do, or to the harm that may be inflicted upon them, for the benefit of others. So the philosophical usage of rights talk reflects the commonsense view that there are limits to what we can justifiably do to an individual for the benefit of society.

To defend the moral rights of animals is to claim that certain ways of treating animals cannot be justified on utilitarian grounds. In the professional philosophical writings cited above, Peter Singer explicitly rejects rights views and adopts a utilitarian stance for dealing with our treatment of nonhuman animals. So the Moses of the animal rights movement is not an animal rights theorist at all.

When the views of animal rights activists are understood this way, in Singer's theoretical terms, animal rights advocates opposed to hunting actually have a lot in common with wildlife managers and hunters who defend hunting as a means to minimizing suffering in wildlife populations. Both factions appeal to the utilitarian tradition in ethics; both believe that it is permissible (at least where nonhuman animals are concerned) to sacrifice (even involuntarily) the life of one individual for the benefit of others, at least where the aggregated benefits to others clearly outweigh the costs to that individual.

Also, the specific conception of happiness the defenders of therapeutic hunting apply to animals is one Singer himself uses, at least in regard to many or most animals. Utilitarianism is the view that right actions maximize aggregate happiness, so it is important for utilitarians to be clear about what happiness consists in. Hedonistic utilitarians define happiness in terms of the presence of pleasure and the absence of pain, where both "pleasure" and "pain" are broadly construed to include not only physical pleasures and pains (e.g., those accompanying orgasms and third-degree burns) but various kinds of pleasant and unpleasant psychological states (e.g., glee, exhilaration, tension, and nervousness). Preference utilitarians define happiness in terms of the satisfaction of preferences (conscious aims, desires, plans, projects), which can, but need not, be accompanied by pleasure.

In *Animal Liberation*, Singer employs a strongly hedonistic conception of happiness. He admits that, "to avoid speciesism," we need not hold that

> it is as wrong to kill a dog as it is to kill a normal human being. . . . [Without being guilty of speciesism] we could still hold that, for instance, it is worse to kill a normal adult human, [or any other being] with a capacity for self-awareness, and the ability to plan for the future and have meaningful relations with others, than it is to kill a mouse, which presumably does not share all of these characteristics. (1990, pp. 18–19)

For this reason, he says that the "wrongness of killing a being is more complicated" than the wrongness of inflicting pain. Nevertheless, he keeps the question of killing "in the background," because

> in the present state of human tyranny over other species the more simple, straightforward principle of equal consideration of pain or pleasure is a sufficient basis for identifying and protesting against all the major abuses of animals that human beings practice. (p. 17)

In *Practical Ethics*, by contrast, Singer devotes four chapters (almost 140 pages) to the "more complicated" question. There he stresses that, with regard to "self-conscious individuals, leading their own lives and wanting to go on living," it is implausible to say that the death of one happy individual is made up for by the birth of an equally happy individual (1993, chap. 5). That is, when dealing with self-conscious beings, preference utilitarianism is more appropriate than hedonistic utilitarianism.

An easy way to clarify Singer's point is with the following example. Suppose I sneak into your bedroom tonight and, without ever disturbing your sleep, kill you by silently releasing an odorless gas. Because you led a relatively happy life (hopefully!) and died painlessly, on a hedonistic conception of happiness, the only sense we can make of the harm I have done to you is in terms of lost future opportunities for pleasure. In the case of human beings, who have complicated desires, intentions, plans, and projects (Bratman 1987 analyzes the subtle differences among these), this seems to be an inadequate accounting of the harm I have done to you. For humans (and any animals with similar cognitive sophistication), a desire-based conception of harm seems more appropriate. But, Singer argues, self-conscious beings are not replaceable. When a being with future-oriented desires dies, those desires remain unsatisfied even if another being is brought into existence and has similar desires satisfied.

Singer cites research that clearly shows, he says, that the great apes (chimpanzees, gorillas, and orangutans) have projects (1993, pp. 111–16, 118, and 132) and, without saying what specific research leads him to these conclusions, that fish and chickens do not have projects (pp. 95, 133) but that a "case can be made, though with varying degrees of confidence, on behalf of whales, dolphins, monkeys, dogs, cats, pigs, seals, bears, cattle, sheep and so on, perhaps even to the point at which it may include all mammals" (p. 132). In chapter 2, I detailed my own reasons for believing that all mammals and birds have desires, or at least rudimentary projects, while fish do not. However, I doubt that self-consciousness, as Singer conceives it, extends nearly so far "down" the "phylogenetic scale" as Singer believes it may. To have the desire to go on living involves not only being self-conscious but also having the concepts of life, death, and self. Although I am prepared to believe that all mammals have desires that transcend the present, nothing I know about the behavior of "lower" mammals (rats and mice, for instance, but also cats and dogs) suggests to me that they have these concepts.

However, it is not necessary, for present purposes, to settle the issue of just how far "down" these concepts go. First, as Singer puts it, blocking the replaceability argument's application to many mammals "raised a very large question mark over the justifiability of a great deal of killing of animals carried out by humans, even when this killing takes place painlessly and without causing suffering to other members of the animal community" (1993, p. 132). But to "raise a very large question mark" is to increase the burden of proof on a justification of killing on preference utilitarian grounds; it is not to rule it out. Second, in the following section, I consider the application of a much stronger view—Tom Regan's rights view—to the hunting question, and there I assume (with Regan) that all mammals have moral rights as he construes them. Because all of the obligatory management species listed above are mammals, this puts a very heavy burden of proof on the defender of therapeutic hunting. My point is that, if even Regan's rights view can be used to defend therapeutic hunting of obligatory management species, then surely a preference utilitarian can defend it as well.

For present purposes, then, let us consider therapeutic hunting from a hedonistic utilitarian perspective. The defense is obvious. Consider the following argument:

(1) We have a moral obligation to minimize pain.
(2) In the case of obligatory management species, more pain would be caused by letting nature take its course than by conducting carefully regulated therapeutic hunts.
(3) Therefore, we are morally obligated to conduct carefully regulated therapeutic hunts of obligatory management species rather than let nature take its course.

Since premise 1 is just a (partial) restatement of the hedonistic utilitarian principle[4] and the argument is valid, premise 2 is the obvious point of controversy.

---

4. Sans the (possibly incoherent) obligation to simultaneously maximize pleasure. See also note 9 below.

But premise 2 states an empirical claim. Thus Singer's disagreement with the hunters and wildlife managers is purely empirical. They agree at the level of moral principle; they disagree only about that principle's application in practice.

Specifically, Singer appears to believe that nonlethal means of population control are (or at least could be made) available and that using them would minimize suffering vis-à-vis therapeutic hunting. Singer has very little to say about hunting specifically. However, at one point in *Practical Ethics*, he clearly indicates that a hedonistic utilitarian could endorse hunting under some circumstances:

> [The replaceability argument is severely] limited in its application. It cannot justify factory farming, where animals do not have pleasant lives. Nor does it *normally* justify the killing of wild animals. A duck shot by a hunter . . . has probably had a pleasant life, but the shooting of a duck does not lead to its replacement by another. *Unless the duck population is at the maximum that can be sustained by the available food supply,* the killing of a duck ends a pleasant life without starting another, and is for that reason wrong on straightforward utilitarian grounds. (1993, pp. 133–34, emphasis added)

Here Singer implicitly admits that the replaceability argument could be used to justify not just therapeutic hunting of obligatory management species but sport hunting of permissive management species. Ducks are not obligatory management species. Ducks do not, in the normal course of events, overshoot the carrying capacity of their habitat in ways that degrade that habitat for future generations of their own and other species. Their management is therefore environmentally permissible but not environmentally obligatory. Nevertheless, a hedonistic utilitarian could endorse sport hunting of permissive management species when, as Singer indicates here, their populations are at or above the carrying capacity of their ranges. As noted above, permissive management species regularly overshoot the carrying capacity of their range by producing more young than their habitat can support, so that every individual killed by a sport hunter is replaced by (because its death makes possible the survival of) another individual. As long as the average death ducks suffer at the hands of hunters involves as little or less pain than the average death surplus ducks would have suffered in nature, pain is minimized.

However, in *Animal Liberation*, Singer writes:

> If it is true that in special circumstances their population grows to such an extent that they damage their own environment and the prospects of their own survival, or that of other animals who share their habitat, then it may be right for humans to take some supervisory action; but obviously if we consider the interests of the animals, this action will not be to allow hunters to kill some animals, inev-

itably wounding others in the process, but rather to reduce the fertility of the animals. (1990, p. 234)[5]

Here Singer admits that therapeutic hunting of obligatory management species is better than letting nature take its course, but he argues that there is yet a better option. Singer appears to be substituting into the above argument a different empirical premise:

(2') By using nonlethal means of controlling populations of obligatory management species, we would minimize suffering visà-vis both letting nature take its course and performing carefully regulated therapeutic hunts,

to reach a different conclusion:

(3') We are morally obligated to use nonlethal means to control populations of obligatory management species.

When all of the learned dust has settled, the disagreement between the Peter Singers of the world and the self-professed advocates of animal welfare among hunters and wildlife managers boils down to an empirical controversy over the effectiveness of nonlethal wildlife population control measures. Both factions agree at the level of moral principle; they disagree over the facts.

My sense is that, at least in the current state of nonlethal wildlife population control, the defenders of hunting have it right. In a retrospective essay written for the centennial of Aldo Leopold's birth, Dale McCullough (the A. Starker Leopold Professor of Wildlife Management at Berkeley) recounts the controversy over deer management on Angel Island in the San Francisco Bay. Under pressure from the San Francisco Society for the Prevention of Cruelty to Animals, the state of California tried both relocating deer and birth control implants. In a follow-up study, McCullough found that 85% of the relocated deer had died within one year of relocation, and the birth control program was abandoned after the society was unable to trap and implant enough females to prevent continued

---

5. Two points about this argument. First, with regard to obligatory management species, it is not just "in special circumstances" that a population of animals "grows to such an extent that they damage their own environment and the prospects of their own survival, or that of other animals who share their habitat." The regularity with which this happens with obligatory management species is what separates them from permissive management species. Second, the choice is not simply between "allow[ing] hunters to kill some animals, inevitably wounding others in the process" and "reduc[ing] the fertility of the animals" by nonlethal means. Hunting regulations could be radically changed to minimize the wounding of animals. For instance, hunting could (in principle) be confined to bait stations with nearby blinds, from which hunters with high caliber, automatic weapons and telescopic sights would kill habituated animals in a selective way (e.g., only does and sicker animals).

population growth (it was estimated that about sixty would need to be implanted). McCullough concluded that "the alternatives to shooting for control of deer populations are expensive, ineffective, and not particularly humane" (1987, p. 121).

For present purposes, however (for assessing convergence of environmentalists' and animal rightists' views on hunting), the point is moot, for two reasons. First, in cases where overpopulation already exists, it is not safe to let all the animals live out their natural lives. If the result of this year's breeding season is a herd already significantly over the carrying capacity of its range, then all the fertility control in the world will not prevent the kind of habitat degradation Singer admits would justify culling some individuals.

Singer's intention, presumably, is to use fertility control to stabilize populations at sustainable levels. But even with regard to such preemptive population control, for present purposes the choice between therapeutic hunting and nonlethal means is moot. If, as the defenders of hunting maintain, hunting is in fact the only effective method of preemptive control, then both environmentalists and hedonistic utilitarians (including both wildlife managers and the Peter Singers of the world) are compelled to support therapeutic hunting. If, on the other hand, effective nonlethal means were currently available, then hedonistic utilitarians would be compelled to support the use of those means rather than therapeutic hunting. Notice, however, that in the latter case the same choice would be open to an environmentalist. For, as noted above, the only hunting environmentalists feel compelled to support is "biologically necessary" hunting. But if nonlethal population control were equally effective, hunting would not be biologically necessary, only the disjunctive choice: hunting or equivalent nonlethal means. That is, an environmentalist would reach conclusion 3":

(3") We are morally obligated to use either (a) therapeutic hunting or (b) biologically equivalent nonlethal means to control populations of obligatory management species.

Just as environmentalists are of two minds with regard to sport hunting that is not also therapeutic, they would be of two minds with regard to the choice between therapeutic hunting and equally effective nonlethal means.

My sense is that the contemporary situation with respect to nonlethal means of deer population management is analogous to the use of hunting as a management tool in Leopold's days. Leopold was skeptical of wildlife managers' ability to control wildlife populations through hunting. He characterized hunting as

a crude, slow, and inaccurate tool, which needs to be supplemented by a precision instrument. The natural aggregation of lions and other predators on an overstocked range, and their natural dispersion from an understocked one, is the only precision instrument known to deer management. ("Report to American Wildlife Institute on the Utah and Oregon Wildlife Units," quoted in Flader 1978, p. 176.)

I suspect that Leopold's skepticism concerning game management derives from his having witnessed the Kaibab irruption of deer in the 1920s and similar population problems in Wisconsin during the 1940s. Decades later, during the 1970s and 1980s, Wisconsin game managers used better censusing techniques and a zone-sensitive permit system (described in Creed et al. 1984) to sustain deer harvests in numbers far exceeding the highest yields ever achieved during Leopold's lifetime. In Leopold's time, it was unusual to harvest over 40,000 animals a year. By the middle 1980s, in contrast, Wisconsin hunters consistently harvested over a quarter of a million deer annually (Wisconsin DNR 1987, pp. 3–4). Certainly other factors were involved (e.g., there was less edge habitat in Wisconsin in the 1940s) but Leopold's dim view of game management probably resulted in large measure from his living during the early days of scientific wildlife management. Nonlethal population control is still slow and crude, as hunting was in Leopold's day. We need to supplement nonlethal methods with a precision instrument (therapeutic hunting, natural predation, or both).

Even if animal rights activists recognized that effective nonlethal population control is not currently available, they might nevertheless choose to go on opposing therapeutic hunting for political purposes. In doing so, they would be practicing brinkmanship: they would be risking disaster (from the perspective of the individual animals involved) in order to force the development of more precise nonlethal techniques of population control. There is no precise way to determine when such brinkmanship is justified, anymore than there is any precise way to determine when civil disobedience or ecosabotage is justified.[6] In both cases, a rough utilitarian calculation is relied upon: in the case of civil disobedience and sabotage, the adverse effects on public order are weighed against the likely benefit of the lawbreaking; in the case of brinkmanship, the risk of a disastrous outcome is weighed against the probability of a breakthrough. However, part of the classic defense of civil disobedience and sabotage is that the conscientious lawbreaker has exhausted available legal means to achieve the goal, and, in the case of therapeutic hunting, activists cannot plausibly claim to have done this. Just as they have successfully forced private companies (such as Mary Kay Cosmetics) and government agencies (such as the NIH) to investigate alternatives to animal models in scientific research and product safety testing, activists could force agencies to put more money into investigations of nonlethal population control methods. So my conclusion is that we should not practice brinkmanship in this case. Therapeutic hunting is a precision tool already available, and, as advocates of animal welfare, we should push for more research into nonlethal means of population control while supplementing nonlethal means with hunting.

6. I employ the analysis of conscientious lawbreaking in Martin 1990, adapting it to the case of brinkmanship.

I do, however, think that precision methods of nonlethal wildlife population control will eventually be developed. Recently, extensive experiments with animals have validated the technique of using genetically engineered viruses to spread infertility among wild animals. By inserting part of the protein sheath from the species' sperm into a virus that spreads easily in the population and then distributing food laced with the virus, Australian researchers hope to eradicate the rabbit, an exotic that has devastated their country. Trials of a similar technique to induce temporary infertility in other species are now under way (Browne 1991). The public in general and animal rights activists in particular are apprehensive of biotechnologies, but this method should, with appropriate caution, be embraced by the animal rights movement as a very promising approach to nonlethal control of wildlife populations.

The above discussion of environmentalists' ambivalent attitudes toward hunting suggests that, if and when effective nonlethal alternatives to therapeutic hunting become available, environmentalists will be split. For some, the availability of nonlethal alternatives will strengthen their opposition to hunting; others will regard the choice between hunting and equally effective nonlethal means as morally moot. For present purposes, what is important is this: animal rights activists operating from a hedonistic utilitarian stance will be compelled to support therapeutic hunting of obligatory management species in the absence of precision, nonlethal methods of wildlife population control. Only when such methods are available must such animal rights activists oppose therapeutic hunting, and then they will oppose it only to embrace a more humane alternative with the same environmental impact.

ANIMAL RIGHTS AND THERAPEUTIC HUNTING

Although Peter Singer's *Animal Liberation* has become "the Bible" of the animal rights movement, Tom Regan's *The Case for Animal Rights* is the best defense available to date of a true animal rights position. It is impossible to do justice to the argument of a 400-page book in a few paragraphs. In what follows, I simply summarize the conclusions Regan reaches, without trying to reproduce his arguments in detail and without critically assessing them apart from their application to the hunting controversy. It is my view that, without resolving the theoretical question of which individuals (if any) have moral rights, we can still hope to make some progress on the practical question of which hunting policy to adopt. Specifically, I argue that in the absence of effective nonlethal means of population control, therapeutic hunting of obligatory management species can be defended from a true animal rights perspective.

According to Regan, there is basically one moral right—the right not to be harmed on the grounds that doing so benefits others—and at least all normal, adult mammals have this basic moral right. In the preface to his most recent anthology, Eugene Hargrove characterizes Regan's position as "more narrowly focused [than Singer's] on protecting the rights of those nonhuman entities with inherent value—those capable of being the subject of a life—which turn out to be mammals and no other forms of life" (1992, p. x). This is misleading. Regan does not deny that any nonmammalian animals have rights. Although he does explicitly restrict the reference of "animal" to "mentally normal mammals of a year or more," Regan does this to avoid the controversy over "line drawing"— that is, the attempt to say precisely where in the phylogenetic scale and where in their ontogeny the mental capacities of animals become so impoverished as to make them incapable of being subjects of a life. And Regan clearly says that he chooses mammals to make sure that his arguments "refer [to] individuals *well beyond* the point where anyone could reasonably 'draw the line' separating those who have the mental abilities in question from those who lack them" (Regan 1983, p. 78). In thus restricting the reference of "animal," he is only acknowledging that the analogical reasoning that would establish that any nonhuman animal has moral rights is strongest in the case of mentally normal adult mammals and becomes progressively weaker as we consider birds and then reptiles, amphibians, and vertebrate fish.

Regan defends two principles for use in deciding whom to harm where it is impossible not to harm someone who has moral rights: the miniride and worse-off principles. The worse-off principle applies where noncomparable harms are involved, and it requires us to avoid harming the worse-off individual. Regan adopts the kind of desire-based conception of harm discussed above in relation to preference utilitarianism. Regan measures harm in terms of the degree to which an individual's capacity to form and satisfy desires has been restricted. The degree of restriction is measured in absolute rather than relative terms. If harm were measured relative to the individual's original capacity to form and satisfy desires rather than in absolute terms, then death would be death wherever it occurs, but Regan reasons that, although death is always the greatest harm any individual can suffer (because it forecloses all opportunity for desire formation and satisfaction), death to a normal human being in the prime of life is noncomparably worse than death to any nonhuman animal in the prime of life because a normal human being's capacity to form and satisfy desires is so much greater. To illustrate the use of the worse-off principle, Regan imagines that five individuals, four humans and a dog, are in a lifeboat that can support only four of them. Because death to any of the human beings would be noncomparably worse than death to the dog, the worse-off principle applies, and it requires us to avoid harming the human beings, who stand to lose the most (1983, pp. 285–86).

The miniride principle applies to cases where comparable harms are involved, and it requires us to harm the few rather than the many. Regan admits that, where it applies, this principle implies the same conclusions as the principle of utility, but he emphasizes that the reasoning is nonutilitarian: the focus is on individuals rather than the aggregate; the miniride principle instructs us to minimize the overriding of individuals' rights rather than to maximize aggregate happiness. Regan says that the rights view (as he calls his position) advocates harming the few (at least where comparable harms are involved), because it respects all individuals equally. To illustrate the miniride principle's application, Regan imagines that a runaway mine train must be sent down one of two shafts and that fifty miners would be killed by sending it down the first shaft but only one by sending it down the second. Because the harms that the various individuals in the example would suffer are comparable, the miniride principle applies, and we are obligated to send the runaway train down the second shaft.

Regan argues that the rights view calls for the abolition of scientific research on animals, hunting and trapping, and all "commercial animal agriculture" (why "commercial," and what this might yet permit, he never explains). He contrasts his views to Singer's in this regard, stressing that, because he is reasoning from a rights-based theory, his conclusions are not contingent upon the facts in the same way as those of a utilitarian like Singer.

At first glance, the prospects for convergence are slim when a true animal rights position like Regan's is opposed to the position of environmentalists. For if having moral rights means that there are certain things that cannot be done to an individual for the sake of the group, and a true animal rights position extends moral rights to animals, then the basic rationale for therapeutic hunting—killing some in order that others may live—appears to be lost. As Regan puts it:

> Put affirmatively, the goal of wildlife managers should be to defend wild animals in the possession of their rights, providing them with the opportunity to live their own life, by their own lights, as best they can, spared that human predation that goes by the name of "sport." . . . If, in reply, we are told that [this] will not minimize the total amount of suffering wild animals will suffer over time, our reply should be that this cannot be the overarching goal of wildlife management, once we take the rights of animals seriously. (1983, p. 357)

Regan appears to be opposed even to therapeutic hunting, and his opposition appears to follow from the attribution of moral rights to animals.

However, Regan never considers the applicability of the miniride principle to hunting. Note that, in the passage quoted above, he focuses on the reasoning presented in defense of therapeutic hunting by wildlife managers. They offer an aggregative, utilitarian argument, and as a rights theorist Regan rejects utilitarian justifications for overriding individual rights. But Regan never considers what the implications would be of applying the miniride principle to the hunting question. Given Regan's conception of harm, death harms all normal individuals of the same species equally. So if it is true that fewer animals will die if therapeutic hunting is used to regulate a wildlife population than if natural attrition is allowed to take its course, then Regan's view implies that therapeutic hunting is not only permissible but a morally mandatory expression of respect for animals' rights.

Similar conclusions could, I think, be reached about certain kinds of medical research using the worse-off principle. Consider AIDS research, for example. (Varner 1994) Given Regan's conception of harm, the harm that death from AIDS is to a normal human being is noncomparably worse than the harm that death from AIDS is to a mouse or even a chimpanzee. So the worse-off principle would, if applicable, imply that nonhuman lives may be sacrificed to save human beings from preventable death.[7] Here again, however, Regan does not apply his principle.

With regard to medical research, Regan bases his abolitionist conclusion primarily on the "special consideration" that "*Risks are not morally transferable to those who do not voluntarily choose to take them*," which, he claims, blocks the application of the worse-off principle (1983, pp. 322 and 377). With respect to the hunting question, Regan might similarly cite a "special consideration" that blocks the application of the miniride principle. He might claim that a violation of an individual's moral rights occurs only when a moral agent is responsible for the harm in question and that, while hunters would be responsible for the deaths of the animals they kill in a therapeutic hunt, no one would be responsible for deaths due to natural attrition. Both Regan and Singer give the following reason for thinking that natural predators do no wrong when they kill. They point out that only the actions of moral agents can be evaluated as right or wrong and that presumably only human beings are moral agents (only human beings are capable of recognizing moral principles and altering their behavior accordingly).

But when a responsible agent knowingly allows nature to take its course, is he or she not responsible by omission for the foreseeable deaths that result? Regan's answer would presumably be no, but this does not seem to me to be a plausible position. Dale Jamieson presents a relevant counterexample. Suppose that a boulder is rolling down a hill toward a hiker and that you can save the hiker by calling out. Jamieson asks, does it make the slightest difference whether the boulder was dislodged by the wind rather than by a would-be murderer? If

---

7. It is worth emphasizing in this context that scientists and agriculturalists who say that, "For an animal rightist, human and animal lives are strictly equal," or "According to animal rights philosophies, 'a rat is a pig is a dog is a boy'," are committing the same intellectual sin they so love to charge animal rights activists with. They attack animal rights philosophies without having troubled to read any of the relevant professional literature (or, if they have read anything, it is only *Animal Liberation*, and they have not read it with careful attention to the philosophical arguments). This is every bit as intellectually irresponsible as a follower of Peter Singer refusing to inform himself or herself about the empirical realities of scientific experimentation or animal agriculture. Singer clearly states that it is not speciesist to hold that killing a normal adult human is as morally serious as killing a mouse, and Regan clearly says that death is a greater harm to a normal adult human than it is to any nonhuman animal. No fair reading of Singer's *Animal Liberation* (let alone his *Practical Ethics*) or Regan's *The Case for Animal Rights* could yield the fundamental misunderstanding of their views commonly repeated by scientists and agriculturalists.

we are not responsible for allowing nature to take its course, then, although you violate the hiker's rights by failing to shout out a warning in the latter case, in the former case you would do the hiker no wrong. But this seems implausible (1990, pp. 351ff.).

There would, I think, be a good reason for not culling overpopulated humans: it is possible for any normal adult human both to understand the gravity of the situation and to alter his or her behavior accordingly. A human being can recognize and act on the obligation of individuals to avoid contributing to overpopulation; a deer, an elephant, or a water buffalo cannot. This gives us a reason for being more reticent about involuntarily culling human beings in a situation of overpopulation. However, I would maintain that this is only a reason for waiting longer before engaging in involuntary culling, for letting the situation get significantly worse before one resorts to such drastic means. Even with regard to humans, it is, I submit, implausible to maintain that the numbers never count. At some point (admittedly unspecifiable in advance), some number of innocent human beings ought to be killed to prevent the foreseeable deaths of some larger number (although again, the minimum required ratio of saved to culled cannot be specified in advance).

Regan claims that the rights view calls for the total abolition of animal research and hunting and that, because he is reasoning from a rights-based theory, his conclusions are not contingent upon the facts in the same way as those of a utilitarian such as Singer (Regan 1983, sec. 6.4). But I argue that a rights view cannot plausibly be insulated from the facts and that, therefore, a true animal rights view need not rule out hunting or research simpliciter. Where therapeutic hunting is the only means available to prevent a large number of foreseeable deaths, a full-blown animal rights position can support therapeutic hunting. And where nonlethal means are available, the case against brinkmanship is stronger from Regan's perspective than it is from Singer's. For, as I argue above, the defense of brinkmanship parallels the classic defense of conscientious lawbreaking, and that defense is in terms of a utilitarian balancing of the magnitude and likelihood of the benefits of lawbreaking (or brinkmanship) against the magnitude and likelihood of the harms of lawbreaking (or brinkmanship). Although I agree with Jamieson that "Regan's theory has serious problems" and that the remedies "would be less clearly in conflict with consequentialist morality" (1990, pp. 349, 362), I think the case against brinkmanship is stronger with Regan. Respect for individuals' rights requires greater aversion to brinkmanship than does the treatment of individuals as receptacles for hedonic utility.

SCRAMBLING POSITIONS ON HUNTING

A critical look at the philosophical foundations of the animal rights movement thus shows that an individual genuinely concerned with animal welfare, and even one who attributes moral rights to nonhuman animals, can support the only kind of hunting environmentalists feel compelled to support, namely therapeutic hunting of obligatory management species.

A critical look at the hunting issue also scrambles the sound-bite-sized positions portrayed in the media. Animal rights activists tend to condemn hunters for being unsportsmanlike, and they tend to condemn management aimed at achieving maximum sustainable yield (MSY) or trophy bucks. However, when it comes to designing an actual therapeutic hunt, advocates of some animal welfare and animal rights views ought to endorse the same management principles that are appropriate to trophy hunting or MSY, and the ideal therapeutic hunt would be anything but sportsmanlike. On the latter point, consider that various unsportsmanlike practices are most conducive to killing specific categories of animals as quickly and painlessly as possible. In the ideal therapeutic hunt, deer would be lured to bait stations near blinds from which sharpshooters with high caliber, automatic weapons would kill them selectively and quickly. This is hardly a paradigm of sportsmanlike hunting, but it is an ideal that serious animal welfarists can endorse.

The former point, about managaging for MSY, cannot be made without a brief discussion of wildlife management principles. For ecologists, the carrying capacity of a deer range is the maximum number of deer the habitat will support on a sustained basis. Wildlife managers, in contrast, have tended to think of carrying capacity in terms of MSY. To avoid confusion, Dale McCullough (1979) advocates calling the former the K carrying capacity of the range, the latter its I carrying capacity. Deer respond to higher population densities by producing fewer fawns (reabsorption of fetuses becomes more common and twins less common), and denser populations are more susceptible to disease and malnutrition. Consequently, maximum yearly recruitment (addition of new adults) occurs well short of K carrying capacity. Management for MSY therefore requires maintenance of deer populations substantially below K carrying capacity, where recruitment rates are highest.

The significance is this. Average individual welfare is higher in populations at I carrying capacity than in populations at K carrying capacity, as evidenced both by more fawns surviving and in higher average weights and reduced parasitism and malnutrition among adults. Only a version of utilitarianism that places preeminent emphasis on the sheer number of animals in the field would imply that management at K carrying capacity is best. But McCullough's model suggests that MSY is achieved short of K carrying capacity, where individual welfare is higher. The ironic result that, when hunters are harvesting the maximum number of animals, they see fewer afield and expend more effort per kill, has occasioned tension between wildlife managers and hunters (McCullough 1984, pp. 219–22). Here is an opportunity for further convergence between pro- and antihunting forces. The policy positions of sport hunters educated to accept management at I carrying capacity for the sake of MSY will converge with those of animal welfare advocates educated to see that MSY management maximizes average individual welfare.

Perhaps more surprising is the fact that management practices that produce the best trophy bucks are more consistent with Regan's rights view than are either management for MSY or K carrying capacity. The largest racks occur on older (four to six years), heavier bucks, and heavier animals have to eat more to maintain themselves. So managing a deer herd to produce the best trophy bucks means sustaining fewer total deer and having fewer "hunting opportunities." As one how-to manual for east Texas deer managers puts it:

> On heavily hunted deer ranges, 90 percent of all the bucks are harvested before they reach four years old. Under these conditions deer do not live long enough to become trophy animals. . . . When managing for maximum quality [read: a preferred trophy], the forked-antlered buck harvest must be at least 30–50 percent less than when managing for maximum harvest. (Spencer 1983, pp. 29, 32)

That is, to produce the best trophy bucks on a range, the population must be maintained below MSY, and this must be accomplished by killing more does and spike bucks[8] and fewer fork-antlered bucks. Although the sex ratio of animals killed changes, if the population is maintained below I carrying capacity and MSY, fewer animals are killed yearly. Here is an opportunity for convergence between the views of trophy hunters and animal rights activists who think like Tom Regan. The miniride principle implies that it is better to manage herds in ways that minimize killing. The trophy management principles just described do just this by emphasizing the taking of does and maintenance of the population below MSY. Enlightened trophy hunters will accept this—the manual just cited is designed to get hunters to stop thinking that good trophy management means buck-only hunting.

It is also possible to endorse the trophy improvement strategy over MSY management from a hedonistic utilitarian perspective. On the assumption that, on average, death is death in hedonistic terms, however it occurs (whether from starvation or human or natural predation), the trophy improvement strategy would minimize pain vis-à-vis the other two management strategies. (Although managing a population at K carrying capacity would involve less hunting than at I carrying capacity, at K carrying capacity, total mortality is greatest.)[9]

8. In bad years or on an already overstocked range, spike bucks (bucks eighteen months or older with unforked antlers) are the result of poor nutrition rather than genetic "inferiority." But, under good conditions such as those obtaining at or below I carrying capacity, bucks who produce spikes as yearlings will never achieve the same degree of antler development as fork-antlered yearlings.

9. Notice, however, that a single-minded emphasis on eliminating pain would seem to imply that hunting a population of sentient creatures to extinction would be a good thing, because this would prevent an infinite amount of pain. Although the hedonistic utilitarian principle as usually formulated involves potentially inconsistent goals (minimize

One further point needs to be emphasized. I define an obligatory management species as one with "a fairly regular tendency to overshoot the carrying capacity of its range," but this does not mean that obligatory management species always need to be hunted. If that were so, then it would not make sense to limit hunting in parks to situations in which hunting becomes "biologically necessary." As McCullough points out:

> Most wildlife biologists and managers can point to situations where deer populations have not been hunted yet do not fluctuate greatly or cause damage to vegetation. Certainly deer reach overpopulation status in some park situations, but the surprising thing is how many parks containing deer populations have no problem. (1984, pp. 239–40)

From an animal welfare or animal rights perspective, the presumption is against hunting. With regard to obligatory management species, it is not unusual for this presumption to be met, although this is not always the case. Ungulates are the classic example of obligatory management species, but even among them there are important variations. In climax-adapted ungulates (such as bison, bighorn sheep, mountain goats, musk ox, and caribou), the magnifying effects of time lags in vegetation damage are less severe than in subclimax ungulates (such as deer, pronghorn antelope, and moose; McCullough 1979, pp. 160 and 172). So the burden of proof necessary to justify therapeutic hunting is more likely to be met with some ungulates (e.g., deer and moose) than with others (e.g., mountain goats or bighorn sheep). The parallel point with regard to permissive management species is that, although they do not degrade their habitats on anything like a regular basis, they can under certain circumstances, and in those circumstances animal rights views can support hunting of them.

PREDATION AND THE PRINCIPLE OF INCLUSIVENESS

My goal in this chapter is to show that views in which preeminent value is placed on the lives of individual sentient creatures can support hunting in those cases where environmentalists feel compelled to support it. Because my own view is not, strictly speaking, an animal rights view, it has remained in the background in this chapter. However, this chapter is the best place to consider, briefly, the implications of my own view on two related subjects: predation in general and the place of predation in human nature in particular.

In chapter 4, I sidestep an issue that could have remarkable implications in the context of wildlife management. In defending the priority-of-ground-projects and priority-of-desires principles, I find it unnecessary to settle the issue of whether a persistent interest's continual satisfaction creates more or less value

---

pain and maximize pleasure), it is thus far preferable to a negative utilitarian principle of simply minimizing pain.

than the serial satisfaction of numerous episodic interests. If the answer to this question is no, then it would appear that on my view individuals are "replaceable" in something like the way they are replaceable on Singer's view. And if this is so, then it would appear that the principle of inclusiveness implies that a predator's life is worth more than the lives of its prey animals.

To see how this is so, suppose that the members of an ungulate species have only one persistent interest, a biological interest in good nutrition, and assume that the satisfaction of this interest creates the same amount of value, irrespective of how long it remains satisfied. Then, if we kill some individuals to make room for others to satisfy this interest, we create more value in the long term than if we let a stable population lead long lives. The described individuals are in this sense replaceable. But now imagine that there is a large predator that can live only on these ungulates, and compare the value of its life to any of its vegetarian prey. To thrive, this predator must continually kill these ungulates. Each time it kills one, it makes way for the satisfaction of another ungulate's interest in good nutrition. Just as the capacity for desire requires the ongoing satisfaction of the lion's share of an individual's biological interests, but not vice versa, the carnivore's survival requires the serial satisfaction of numerous of these ungulates' one persistent interest, but not vice versa. Apparently, the predator's interest in good nutrition is more inclusive than its prey's interest in good nutrition.

The endorsement of this result would be something of a mixed blessing for my view. On the one hand, it seems ironic for an individualist ethical stance to support the conclusion that there is more value in the life of an individual that continuously kills other conscious individuals to survive than in the life of a vegetarian. On the other hand, it would provide further support for one plank in the environmentalist agenda, namely the goal of restoring locally extinct predators.

However, without being able to assign comparative magnitudes to the satisfaction of the interests in question, I do not know how to settle the issue of whether the continuous satisfaction of a persistent interest creates more or less value than the serial satisfaction of numerous episodic interests. So I must leave this issue unresolved.

I conclude with a short comment on the value of predation to humans specifically. It has long been thought that the remarkable cognitive capacities of humans evolved under selection for predation (see, for instance, Richards 1987 and Donald 1991). Suppose that this is the case; suppose, that is, that predation is natural for human beings in the sense that any adaptive trait that human beings displayed during their evolutionary emergence as a species is natural for them. What would this imply about the morality of hunting? Nothing decisive, for two reasons.

First, it is in the same sense natural for us to make stone tools and defecate in the woods, but no one argues that we should continue to do these things just because they are natural. Showing that something is natural in this sense does not suffice to show that it is morally permissible, let alone in some sense morally obligatory or at least exemplary. No one would accept such a rationale for sexism or bigotry, if those could be shown to be equally natural in this sense.

Of course the sophisticated defenders of hunting do not stop with such a crude argument. They go further and insist that, of all the activities that are natural for us, hunting allows us to experience and celebrate our evolutionary roots in a way that nothing else does. José Ortega y Gasset (1985) and Paul Shepard (1973), for example, have eloquently described the way tracking, killing, and consuming a large mammal exercises our distinctive faculties in an especially inclusive and intensive way.

This argument from the naturalness of hunting employs a perfectly familiar and reputable sense of the term "natural." However, there is an equally familiar and reputable sense of the term in which the most natural thing for us to do is question the morality of the hunting that is natural for us in the first sense of the term. Aristotle employed this sense of "natural" in the famous *ergon* argument of his *Nicomachean Ethics*. Roughly, Aristotle says that the exercise of a capacity is the *ergon* of a species if it is the capacity the species shares with no other species. What is natural for humans in this sense is the exercise of whatever capacity distinguishes us from all other animals. Aristotle argued that reasoning is *ergon* for humans (*Nicomachean Ethics* 1098a). For the reasons given in chapter 2, I doubt this. In light of contemporary ethology, the capacity for moral agency is a more plausible candidate for a uniquely human function than is the capacity for reason. But this means that reflecting on the morality of our actions, including actions that are "natural" in the previously considered sense of the term, is as natural for us to do as anything. So, at least with the theoretical puzzle about replaceability put to one side, acknowledging that hunting is in one sense natural for humans implies nothing compelling about the morality of hunting.

What of meat eating in general? Singer's, Regan's, and my own principles all imply that, if human beings must eat some meat or at least some meat by-products in order to thrive, then they are justified in doing so. This could well be the case, especially for individuals with high metabolic requirements, pregnant or lactating women and growing children, for example. The evidence is indecisive, involving complex issues in nutrition science.[10] It may also turn out that animals must have a role in sustainable agriculture, especially in the developing nations, where animals provide not only food but draft power and fertilizer. For such reasons, some form of animal agriculture may turn out to be a necessary feature of human society. Be that as it may, the more benign forms are to be preferred. The ideal to be approximated is a systematic harmony of interests.

10. For a comprehensive overview, see the special issue of the *Journal of Agricultural and Environmental Ethics*, "Might Morality Require Veganism?" edited by Gary Comstock (1994).

CHAPTER SIX

Justifying the Environmentalist Agenda

MY VIEW can fairly be characterized as anthropocentric, at least in one sense. As I use the terms, a view is valuationally anthropocentric just in case it involves attribution of intrinsic value only to human beings, and a view is axiologically anthropocentric if its principles favor at least some human interests when these are in conflict with the interests of nonhumans. My view is not valuationally anthropocentric, because it involves attribution of intrinsic value to the satisfaction of every interest of every living thing, whatever its species. However, my view can fairly be described as axiologically anthropocentric, for principle P2' is that the satisfaction of a ground project creates more value than the satisfaction of any other kind of interest, and I am willing to admit that only human beings have ground projects. And, because I embrace no aggregative principle of obligation, my view provides no way of arguing that a human being's ground project ought to be doomed despite the fact that, considered in isolation, its satisfaction creates preeminent value. That is, in the axiology of my view (the principles I defend in chapter 4), pride of place is given to certain interests that only humans have.

As detailed in the introduction, anthropocentric views have gotten a lot of bad press in environmental ethics, and, because the preferred alternative is holism, a view like mine seems to have two strikes against it: it is a version of individualism and, moreover, it is anthropocentric, at least axiologically. In this chapter, I argue that such a view can support the general goals mentioned on the environmentalist agenda. As formulated in the introduction, these goals include:

1. preservation of species, wilderness, and special habitats such as wetlands, estuaries, rain forests, and deserts;
2. reintroduction of locally extinct species including large predators, removal of exotic species, and adaptation of agricultural and landscaping practices to the local biota;

3. substantial reductions in air and water pollution; and
4. substantial reduction of the global human population.

Can only holists support such goals? Surely not. Consider, as a first approximation, this argument:

(1) We have a general duty to preserve the context in which future generations of humans can pursue their most important interests; these interests are of overriding moral importance.
(2) Safeguarding future generations' pursuit of these interests requires us to pursue the goals listed on the environmentalist agenda.
(3) Therefore, we ought to attempt to reverse human population growth, and so on.

At the end of this chapter, I formulate the specific version of this argument that my own axiologically anthropocentric version of biocentric individualism implies. Here, let me just sketch the reasons this is an argument that anthropocentrists, animal rights activists, and biocentric individualists can all agree with.

As I say in chapter 4, any plausible version of biocentric individualism or of an animal rights view must embrace a principle like P2' and thus be axiologically anthropocentric. In fact, even a valuationally anthropocentric view will be implausible unless it adopts such a principle, for it would be implausible to place all human interests on a par. This is why anthropocentrists, animal rights activists, and biocentric individualists can all agree on the general axiological point expressed in the first premise of the above argument.

Once a principle like P2' is embraced, however, a general consensus on the goals on the environmentalist agenda will emerge if the general empirical claim in premise 2 is also embraced by all. In this chapter, I spell out reasons for thinking that this empirical claim is true. I begin with a general look at the distinction between preservation and conservation, and I argue that increasingly these two interpenetrate in practice, that even the classic cases of "preservation" (wilderness areas and the larger, more pristine national parks) require active management. I then turn to a detailed discussion of Aldo Leopold's life and the evolution of his land management philosophy. I pay special attention to its implications for the management of more-developed areas like national forests and farms. There too, I argue, conservation and preservation increasingly interpenetrate: conservation (i.e., "wise use") increasingly requires the preservation of remaining tracts of special habitats (like wetlands), critical habitat for endangered species, and "wilder" areas. I close with an overview of how this interpenetration of conservation and preservation requires pursuit of the goals on the environmentalist agenda.

Agreement on a general argument like the one above will not settle all (or even, I suspect, very many) specific policy questions. Continued growth of the world's human population is fairly clearly at odds with pursuit of the other goals on the environmentalist agenda. However, where specifically should the population be stabilized? Ten billion? Five billion? One billion? And where specifically should reductions come? Population growth rates are lower in the industrialized nations, but per capita consumption of natural resources is much higher, so where is it more important to reduce the population? Similarly, as conservation increasingly requires preservation, we must increasingly reintroduce locally extinct species. But which ones? And where? These are specific policy questions that are more raised than answered by agreement on the above argument. Still, the above argument indicates that divergent value systems will converge at the level of policy as evidence accumulates in support of the second premise—that safeguarding the ability of future generations to pursue their most important interests requires us to pursue the goals listed on the environmentalist agenda. As Bryan Norton puts it:

> Long-sighted anthropocentrists and ecocentrists tend to adopt more and more similar policies as scientific evidence is gathered, because both value systems— *and several others as well*—point toward the common-denominator objective of protecting ecological contexts. (1991, p. 246, emphasis added)

In the preceding chapter, I argue that animal rights views are one of these "several other" views. My point in this chapter is that an axiologically anthropocentric biocentric individualism is too.

CONSERVATION IN THE WILDERNESS

The title of this section may sound like an oxymoron. In terms of both their motives and their methods, conservation and preservation commonly are thought to be worlds apart, and wilderness is the place to practice preservation, not conservation.

"Conservation" commonly is taken to refer to intelligent use of resources in the service of human wants and needs, whereas "preservation" commonly is taken to refer to leaving nature alone for its own sake. So, in terms of their underlying moral motives, conservationists are thought to be anthropocentrists, whereas preservationists are biocentrists.

There is also a tendency to distinguish conservation from preservation in terms of how "natural" the practice of preservation is in contrast to the practice of conservation. We tend to think of preservation as leaving the landscape alone, in its "natural" state, and of conservation as alteration intended to produce a landscape that is less natural but more useful to humans. The paradigm of preservation is a wilderness or one of the larger, more pristine national parks, whereas the paradigm of conservation is a national forest or a well-run farm. Preservationists see in the former a management style that respects nature by leaving it alone; conservationists see in the latter a management style that uses nature intelligently and efficiently. Preservationists, we often hear, want to "lock up" vast landscapes and prevent all productive human uses of them because they attribute intrinsic value to nature. Conservationists, we hear, want to develop all lands because they value nature only instrumentally. I do not think conservation and preservation are as far apart, motivationally or methodologically, as the received view would have it.

Arguing from a pragmatist perspective, Bryan Norton claims that, despite such deep-seated differences in their value commitments, people can agree at the level of policy; that is, they can agree about what ought to be done while disagreeing about why. To emphasize this, Norton distinguishes between convergence, agreement at the level of policy despite underlying differences at the level of moral principle, and full-blown consensus—that is, agreement at both levels. By "the convergence hypothesis" Norton (1991) means (as he puts it) the "faith" that growing scientific understanding of ecological systems leads to convergence on broad policy goals among people with very different underlying moral philosophies.

In *Toward Unity among Environmentalists* (1991), Norton argues that environmentalists (and environmental philosophers) should stop thinking in terms of the anthropocentrism–biocentrism dichotomy and instead concentrate on broad areas of policy agreement. For example, he argues that, at least at this time, enlightened anthropocentrists and holists can agree that a patchwork of diverse habitats should be preserved, remaining wildlands protected from development, human population growth curbed, pollution reduced, and so forth. Norton says that in his argument he

> recognizes the crucial role of creative, self-organizing systems in supporting human economic, recreational, aesthetic, and spiritual values. Because self-organizing systems maintain a degree of stable functioning across time, they provide a sufficiently stable context to which human individuals and cultures can adapt their practices. (1992, p. 24)

Because of the "centrality and intransigence of scaling problems" (p. 34), Norton doubts that adequate indicators of ecosystemic health are currently available, but he stresses the general importance of what he calls "total diversity"—roughly, a combination of α-diversity (diversity of species) and β-diversity (diversity of habitats across a landscape [1987])—and the preservation of normal rates of change in environmental systems (1991). He therefore unpacks the duty to preserve natural variety in terms of preserving (or, where necessary, restoring) the integrity of ecosystems. He says that

> An ecosystem has maintained its integrity . . . if it retains (1) the total diversity of the system—the sum total of the species and associations that have held sway historically—and (2) the systematic organization which maintains that diversity,

including, especially, the system's multiple layers of complexity through time. (1992, p. 26)

If future generations of human beings can fulfill their most important interests only against a background of relatively intact ecosystems, then on purely anthropocentric grounds we ought to preserve relatively intact ecosystems.

For such reasons, Norton suggests in an early paper titled "Conservation and Preservation: A Conceptual Rehabilitation" that we reconceive the distinction in terms of general policy goals rather than in terms of motivations or moral principles. He suggests these alternative definitions: "*to conserve* a resource . . . is to use it wisely, with the goal of maintaining its future availability or productivity," and "*To preserve* is to protect an ecosystem . . . to the extent possible, from the disruptions attendant upon it from human use." So conceived, "Conservation and preservation are different activities, which might result from varied and complex motives" (1987, pp. 200–201). That is, there can be human-centered reasons for preserving more natural ecosystems, and, by thinking of preservation in these terms, environmentalists are freed from having to base their arguments on appeals to the rights or intrinsic value of nonhuman organisms or ecosystems.

With regard to the associated tendency to distinguish conservation from preservation in terms of relative "naturalness" of management styles, there is a crucial ambiguity. In one familiar sense of the word, a landscape is "natural" to the extent that its existence and functioning is not an artifact—that is, to the extent that it does not result largely or entirely from conscious manipulation by human beings. However, in an equally familiar but importantly different sense of the term, a landscape is "natural" to the extent that it approximates presettlement conditions. This is the sense of a "natural" landscape codified in the 1963 Leopold report (the lead author of which was Aldo Leopold's son A. Starker Leopold) as the goal of ecosystem management in U.S. national parks. The report contains a summary of what was already widely understood to be the overarching goal of ecosystem management in the parks:

> As a primary goal, we would recommend that the biotic associations within each park be maintained, or where necessary recreated, as nearly as possible in the condition that prevailed when the area was first visited by the white man. A national park should be a vignette of primitive America. (A. Starker Leopold et al. 1963, p. 32)

But the authors of the report emphasize that management to achieve a result that is natural in this sense—let us call it natural in result—may require management that ensures the resulting ecosystem is highly unnatural in genesis.

If a "preserved" landscape were required to be natural in both genesis and result, then preservation would be impossible in most instances. Indeed, in a widely cited book, Bill McKibben argues that human modification of the biosphere is already so pervasive that no landscape is any longer natural in origin:

We have killed off nature—that world entirely independent of us which was here before we arrived and which encircled and supported our human society. There's still something out there, though; in the place of the old nature rears up a new "nature" of our own devising. It is like the old nature in that it makes its points through what we think of as natural processes (rain, wind, heat), but it offers none of the consolations—the retreat from the human world, the sense of permanence, and even of eternity. Instead, each cubic yard of air, each square foot of soil, is stamped indelibly with our crude imprint, our X. (1989, p. 96)

McKibben's point is exaggerated. In neither sense of "natural" is naturalness an all-or-nothing thing. Landscapes lie on a continuum of naturalness, with the extreme cases being obviously and importantly different from each other. Manhattan is at one extreme, and Antarctica at the other, in both senses of the term. And this is so despite the fact that there are traces of various pollutants in the Antarctic icecap (so that Antarctica is, in a marginal sense, an artifact) and traces of pre-Columbian flora and fauna in Manhattan (so that Central Park—a landscape that was constructed literally from the ground up in the 1860s—is, in a marginal sense, natural in result).

More interesting than McKibben's worry about the artifactuality of all the earth is the practical irony that, in most places today, to achieve a landscape that is more natural in result (that more closely approximates presettlement conditions), techniques must be used that ensure the landscape is more unnatural in genesis (which makes it more artifactual). Sometimes (although certainly not always), this artifactuality is short term. Presumably some ecological restorations become autogenic, requiring no intervention after a few years. In such cases, we might say that the landscape becomes increasingly natural in genesis as time passes beyond the restorative intervention. In other cases, however, ongoing conscious management is required to maintain presettlement conditions. This is true of restored oak savannahs, for example, where prescribed burning is necessary to prevent succession to a continuous forest that would be less natural in result than the oak savannah.

This irony should not surprise us, however. As the Leopold report indicates, one of the major influences on national park ecosystems in pre-Columbian times, which is now missing from them and must be compensated for to achieve a more natural result, is aboriginal Americans. "Presettlement" in the Leopold report means prior to occupation by Europeans. Throughout North America, evidence indicates that aboriginal occupants heavily modified their environment using fire. For example, New England aboriginals used fire extensively (Cronon 1983, pp. 49–51) and a tree scar study in the Northern Rockies suggests that lightning-caused fires may have accounted for only about half of the fires that occurred in pre-Columbian times (Barrett 1981).

The influence of aboriginal Americans on pre-Columbian ecosystems suggests another way in which the preservation–conservation distinction is a false dichotomy. The baseline, pre-Columbian ecosystems against which we measure the naturalness of the result were themselves the result of extensive human manipulation. We cannot be certain to what extent this manipulation was conscious. Aboriginal Americans had many reasons for burning in various places: to drive or concentrate game to make it easier to kill; to create conditions favorable to gatherable foods such as strawberries, blackberries, and raspberries; to create more hospitable camping areas; to control forest undergrowth to make travel easier and to locate game; to prevent woodlands encroaching on hillocks useful for defensive purposes; to open land for swidden agriculture; to increase the "edge effect" that favors denser ungulate populations (see Chase 1986, pp. 92–97, and Cronon 1983, pp. 50–51, and the references cited there). Burning for many of these reasons would have been done with the goal of affecting the landscape kept consciously in mind, although some burning may have become ritualized and the conscious tie to landscape modification lost. We do not know. What is clear, however, is that today, in most cases, to achieve a result that is more natural in the sense of more closely approximating pre-Columbian conditions, we must use the kind of consciously calculated techniques that ensure that the intended result is highly artifactual and thus highly unnatural in origins.

With regard to areas such as national parks and wilderness, then, the conservation–preservation distinction, when drawn in terms of a relatively "natural" management regime, presents us with a false dichotomy. To me, the most fascinating thing about Aldo Leopold's *A Sand County Almanac* has always been the way in which he turned this basic insight on its head in relation to heavily managed areas such as national forests, farms, and (at least implicitly) towns and cities. I have just shown how, in relatively pristine areas, preservation increasingly requires some admixture of the techniques associated with conservation. Leopold added the insight that in highly managed areas, conservation increasingly requires simultaneous pursuit of the goals of preservation. After discussing the interpretation of Leopold's moral philosophy in the next section, I turn to a discussion of this land management philosophy. Leopold's land management philosophy illustrates better than anything else I have read how conservation and preservation interpenetrate in a way that supports the empirical claim underlying the environmentalist agenda.

INTERPRETING LEOPOLD'S LAND ETHIC

Aldo Leopold's *A Sand County Almanac* (1949) was not an instant classic. When published by Oxford the year after Leopold died fighting a grass fire on a neighbor's property, it received scant notice. However, with the flowering of the modern environmental movement in the late 1960s and the issuance of a trade paperback edition by Ballantine in 1966, sales of the book took off and an enormous number of people began to claim Leopold as their philosophical inspiration.

In his widely reprinted "Triangular Affair" essay (1980), J. Baird Callicott, the leading philosophical expositor of Leopold, used "The Land Ethic" as a sort of ostensive definition of "environmental ethics." *Audubon* magazine called Leopold the "patron saint of the modern environmental movement," and biologist Ren Dubois called the book "The Holy Writ of American Conservation" (cited in Nash 1989, p. 63). The renowned Secretary of the Interior Stewart Udall said that "if asked to select a single volume which contains a noble elegy for the American earth and a plea for a new land ethic, most of us at Interior would vote for Aldo Leopold's *A Sand County Almanac*" (quoted in Nash 1989, p. 63). And the Clinton administration's Secretary of the Interior, Bruce Babbitt, wrote an essay for the 100th anniversary of Leopold's birth in which he claimed Leopold as a great inspiration in his own thinking (Babbitt 1987).

More interesting than the sheer number of people who claim to have been inspired by Leopold is the political range of people who claim Leopold as their philosophical inspiration. Dave Foreman, cofounder of the radical environmental group Earth First!, called *Sand County* "the most important book ever written" (quoted in Nash 1989, p. 63). At the opposite end of the preservation–conservation spectrum is Joseph Schuster, former head of the Texas A&M Department of Rangeland Ecology and Mangement. When his son left the practice of law in Amarillo to return to Texas A&M for a graduate degree in the department, Schuster sent his son a copy of *Sand County* and told him that it would be "his *Bible*" while studying in the department (Kent Schuster, personal communication with the author).

A book that Dave Foreman and Joe Schuster claim as their philosophical inspiration has to be one that appeals to very pluralistic motivations, and this is indeed the case. At one extreme, philosophically, is the most often-quoted passage from the book, Leopold's summary statement of the land ethic:

> quit thinking about decent land-use as solely an economic problem. Examine each question in terms of what is ethically and esthetically right, as well as what is economically expedient. A thing is right when it tends to preserve the integrity, stability, and beauty of the biotic community. It is wrong when it tends otherwise. (1949, 224–25)

Taken literally, the penultimate sentence of this passage appears to define right and wrong practices solely in terms of their effects on biotic communities. This strongly holistic theme has been played up by environmentalists who, like Foreman, call for relatively radical restructuring and by Callicott. Callicott then argues that ecological and evolutionary science are so transforming our conception of community that we are coming to perceive every other living thing as a member of a common biotic community to which our natural sentiments therefore extend. Callicott sees Leopold's discussion of the "community concept" in "The Land Ethic," and even his highly anthropomorphic descriptions of animals in the shack sketches, as Leopold's way of helping his readers adopt a nonanthropocentric perspective in ethics.

However, it is easy to find places in *Sand County* where Leopold appeals to the collective self-interest of human beings. In the above passage, for example, he says that the well-being of the biotic community should be considered "as well as" economic expediency, and elsewhere he explicitly denies that economic considerations can be entirely ignored: "It of course goes without saying that economic feasibility limits the tether of what can or cannot be done for land. It always has and it always will" (1949, p. 225). He repeatedly affirms the right of humans to modify and use land: "A land ethic of course cannot prevent the alteration, management, and use of these 'resources,' but it does affirm their right to continued existence, and, at least in spots, their continued existence in a natural state" (p. 204). Leopold's statement at the conclusion of "The Land Ethic," that the steam shovel "has many good points" but "we are in need of gentler and more objective[1] criteria for its successful use," suggests that pursuit of our own good often backfires because we overuse technologies, modifying our environment beyond the point that is good for us. A similar theme is evident in the opening pages of the essay. Having characterized an ethic as "a mode of guidance [where] the path of social expediency is not discernible to the average individual . . . a kind of community instinct in-the-making" (p. 203), when Leopold says that an extension of ethics to the nonhuman world is "an ecological necessity," he appears to be making the same point: pursuit of our own good often backfires because we overuse technologies, modifying our environment beyond the point that doing so is good for us.

How are we to explain Leopold's dovetailing of anthropocentric and biocentric considerations? One possibility is that Leopold is articulating a kind of self-effacing anthropocentrism, the view that, on purely anthropocentric grounds, we ought to quit thinking like anthropocentrists, at least on a day-to-day basis. A number of utilitarian ethicists have made similar claims. Henry Sidgwick, for example, argues that, under certain sociological conditions (e.g., when the society at large is highly antagonistic to utilitarianism), consistent utilitarians should offer, publicly, nonutilitarian arguments for conclusions they had reached on utilitarian grounds privately (1874, bk. 4, chap. 4). More apropos the current subject, British moral philosopher R. M. Hare argues that in daily life we are so

---

1. Leopold's use of the term "objective" here, in the passages quoted below during discussion of his textbook *Game Management*, and elsewhere (e.g., the essay "Thinking Like a Mountain": "Only the mountain has lived long enough to listen objectively to the howl of the wolf" [1949, p. 129]) is curious. As best I can tell, by "objective" he means "sustainable," but there is no precedent in the *Oxford English Dictionary* for this usage. Perhaps he is assuming the pragmatist conception of truth discussed below in the text and playing off of the parallel between "objective" and "true."

likely to "cook the data" to suit our own interests that a consistent utilitarian would adopt "intuitive level" moral principles much more simple and general than those a utilitarian would endorse under ideal epistemic and motivational conditions (1981, p. 38). For example, to combat the tendency to see one's case as the exception, one might adopt an intuitive level moral principle of never committing adultery, even though careful critical thinking in a quiet moment would lead one to say that there are justifiable exceptions. Similarly, the structure of *Sand County*—which begins with the highly anthropomorphic shack sketches—can be viewed as an attempt on Leopold's part to "trick" the reader into thinking nonanthropocentrically for similar reasons. In theory, enlightened anthropocentrists would not modify their environment beyond the point that doing so is good for them, but in practice people thinking anthropocentrically will in fact do so. On this reading, Callicott would be right that Leopold's anthropomorphic shack sketches are an encouragement to think in the biocentric way expressed in his summary statement of the land ethic. It is a sort of deception required as a hedge against human intemperance.

This reading probably attributes unnecessary subtlety (and subterfuge) to Leopold in *Sand County*. Bryan Norton has proposed a much simpler interpretation supported both by the text of *Sand County* and by certain biographical facts about Leopold. Norton notes that the American pragmatist philosopher Arthur Twining Hadley was president of Yale during Leopold's time there. Hadley offers a pragmatist, evolutionary account of belief in terms very close to those used by Leopold in the opening sections of "The Land Ethic." Hadley writes: "I do not mean that we should consciously adopt a belief because it is useful to us, as James seems to imply. I would rather take the ground that we hold the belief that has preserved our fathers as an intuition and act on it as an instinct." With regard to ethics, specifically, he writes: "The criterion which shows whether a thing is right or wrong is its permanence. Survival is not merely the characteristic of right; it is the test of right" (both quoted in Norton 1988, p. 95). Although these passages are quoted from Hadley's most philosophical book, which was published in 1913, several years after Leopold left Yale, Leopold probably was exposed to Hadley's general pragmatist conception of truth while at Yale and probably saw a review of Hadley's book in the *Yale Review* in 1913. This is confirmed in a 1923 paper, in which Leopold refers explicitly, albeit parenthetically, to Hadley: "(How happy a definition is Hadley's which states, 'Truth is that which prevails in the long run'!)." The reference occurs in a section subtitled "Conservation as a Moral Issue," in which Leopold flirts with biocentrism in ethics as an alternative to anthropocentrism but says that he "will not dispute the point" (Leopold 1979, pp. 141, 140). Norton's hypothesis is that Leopold's views on ethics did not change between his early days in the Southwest and his mature days in Wisconsin. Rather, Leopold was a pragmatist from the beginning, and his professional experiences convinced him that he did not have to choose between an enlightened anthropocentrism and biocentrism. He saw that the implications of the two converge in practice and that each is equally true in pragmatist terms. This would explain the simultaneous presence in *Sand County* of biocentric and anthropocentric language. Also, in the opening sections of "The Land Ethic," Leopold characterizes ethics in terms reminiscent of Hadley's evolutionary account, as "a kind of community instinct in-the-making" (1949, p. 203). (Note also the point about Leopold's use of the term "objective" in n. 1 above.)

Norton's interpretation of Leopold fits Leopold's literary corpus nicely and is grounded squarely on the details of Leopold's life at Yale and as a professional land manager. It also illustrates the first way in which preservation and conservation converge: one can endorse a more preservationist stance from either an anthropocentric or a biocentric stance. Although Leopold did not oppose development per se, he cautioned that even in purely anthropocentric terms it sometimes makes sense to leave areas undeveloped. And a look at the specific land management strategies that Leopold developed over the course of his life illustrates how, even in highly managed areas, conservation increasingly requires simultaneous pursuit of the goals of preservation.

Preservation on the Farm

The title of this section again may seem to be an oxymoron. A farm is the paradigm example of an anthropogenic environment. But Leopold argues that not only forests but also farms and ranches, especially those in less resilient ecosystems such as the arid Southwestern United States, should be part of a general biodiversity management program—that is, both forests and farms and ranches should be managed for multiple use and sustained yield. This outlook evolved in the course of his professional career as a land manager.

When Leopold graduated from the Yale University School of Forestry in 1909, he was one of the first professionally trained foresters in the United States. The school, which had been endowed just nine years earlier by the Gifford Pinchot family, was the first in the United States. The school reflected the anthropocentric, utilitarian philosophy of the U.S. Forest Service, which Pinchot headed at the time. It emphasized economic analysis as a policy-setting tool and predator extermination as a game management technique. Leopold rose quickly through the Forest Service ranks to become supervisor of the Carson National Forest in 1912. There he began an aggressive and very successful program of predator extermination. In three years (from 1917 to 1920), the wolf population of New Mexico dropped from 300 to 30. Leopold defended the program with economic arguments. He calculated the value of deer killed in New Mexico in 1915 at $43,296, assuming $0.15 per pound for the meat obtained by hunters, $1 per hide, and an average of $50 in recreational expenses (transportation, provisions, licenses, and equipment) per kill. At the time, only about 700 deer were being harvested by hunters annually in New Mexico, but Leopold estimated that 100 remaining mountain lions were responsible for up to 3000 kills per year, representing a dramatic economic loss to the state (Flader 1978, p. 60). While still aggressively advocating predator elimination, Leopold was gleaning from his experience with Southwestern watersheds some of the basic lessons that later would lead him to oppose predator extermination in his mature management philosophy.

At the time, it was thought that there had been no increase in erosion rates on Southwestern watersheds since settlement by Europeans and that visible erosion was part of an ongoing geological process. However, when Leopold compared contemporary conditions in mountain valleys to the oldest settlers' memories of initial conditions there, he found that twenty-seven out of thirty were significantly degraded. Leopold argued that rates of erosion were higher because plant communities that had previously anchored stream courses had been destroyed by range cattle. In his 1923 paper "Some Fundamentals of Conservation in the Southwest," Leopold recommended managing cattle with the goal of restoring native plant communities on watersheds and in stream beds. Leopold argued that the "fabric of prosperity" was unraveling because the fragile ecosystems of the arid Southwest could not absorb the degree and rapidity of the changes they were undergoing.

The lessons Leopold drew from his experience with Southwestern watersheds informed his thinking until the end. First and foremost,

(1) We do not (and probably cannot) know enough to tinker precisely with ecosystems, designing them to get just the outcomes we want.

This is why, as he puts it in *Sand County*, "the conqueror role is eventually self-defeating" (1949, p. 204): "The ordinary citizen today assumes that science knows what makes the community clock tick; the scientist is equally sure that he does not. He knows that the biotic mechanism is so complex that its workings may never be fully understood" (205). Second,

(2) Regions vary in resilience, in the amount of human modification they can sustain without losing their long-term fecundity.

In *Sand County*, Leopold compares the arid Southwest to Western Europe and Japan. He notes that Western Europe and Japan have absorbed dramatic modification without losing their fecundity, whereas the Southwest was in decline after less than half a century of exploitation. "Biotas seem to differ in their capacity to sustain violent conversion," he concludes (p. 218).

(3) In all regions, the original, naturally evolved biota maintain long-term fecundity; introduced species may or may not.

This is repeated in the section of "The Land Ethic" on "The Biotic Pyramid," in which Leopold observes that land "is not merely soil; it is a fountain of energy flowing through a circuit of soils, plants, and animals" (p. 216) and "the native plants and animals kept the energy circuit open; others may or may not" (p. 218). From the foregoing points, Leopold concluded that

(4) In more fragile regions, a greater effort should be made to adopt agricultural and landscaping practices that mimic or approximate the original, naturally evolved ecosystems of the region.

And:

(5) In all regions, samples of the original biota (including all native species) should be preserved.

Thus he writes in *Sand County* that a land ethic "affirms" the "right" of all species "to continued existence, and, at least in spots, their continued existence in a natural state" (p. 204), and he warns (again) that, in more-fragile regions like the Southwest, less drastic modification of native ecosystems is absorbable (p. 206). Lessons 4 and 5 are the heart of Leopold's mature land management philosophy. His mature view of large predators reflects their extension from watershed management to game management.

Leopold moved to the Madison Forest Products Research Center in 1924 and, after working as a freelance consultant during the early years of the Great Depression, was appointed to the first chair of game management at the University of Wisconsin–Madison in 1933. That same year, his textbook *Game Management* appeared. In it, Leopold presents a systematic picture of game herd population dynamics and a very optimistic view of managers' ability to maximize harvests by minimizing predation. He says that intelligent manipulation of a few variables would allow humans to "substitute a new and objective equilibrium for any natural one that civilization might have destroyed" (1933, p. 26). Indeed,

> Leopold estimated that it would require five man-years of rudimentary research on deer in Wisconsin to identify and weigh the factors inhibiting their increase, to test the techniques of control on a sample area, and to run down "side lines." . . . In view of the hundreds of man-years of research that have been devoted to deer and other game species in Wisconsin since the 1940's, Leopold's estimate may seem naive. But it is a measure of his optimism at the time about increasing game populations by means of relatively simple environmental controls. (Flader 1978, p. 137)

But, by 1933, Leopold's experience with a series of population irruptions on newly wolfless ranges was already tempering his optimism.

During the middle 1920s, the celebrated irruption of the deer herd on the Kaibab Plateau north of the Grand Canyon occurred. And, during the 1930s and

1940s, Leopold battled Wisconsin sportsmen and legislators over management of Wisconsin's deer. Leopold believed the Wisconsin herd was overshooting the carrying capacity of its range and that it would, if not drastically reduced, crash disastrously like the Kaibab herd before it. In a decade when Wisconsin deer harvests were averaging only about 15,000–30,000 a year, Leopold successfully campaigned for a split season in 1943, resulting in a harvest of 128,000 deer (Wisconsin DNR 1987, p. 3). Many hunters were outraged; one hunters' group referred to the season as the "infamous and bloody 1943 deer slaughter" (quoted in Flader 1978, p. 202). Leopold drafted "Thinking Like a Mountain" in April of 1944 (Meine 1988, p. 450).

The shift in Leopold's thinking about predators is dramatically illustrated in a lecture he gave at Beloit College in 1936, only three years after the publication of *Game Management*. In it, he says, "Wildlife management . . . has already admitted its inability to replace natural equilibria with artificial ones" (Leopold 1990, p. 331), which is a direct contradiction of the passage quoted above. The depth of his growing technological pessimism is reflected in a letter of 1941:

> Hunting is a crude, slow, and inaccurate tool, which needs to be supplemented by a precision instrument. The natural aggregation of lions and other predators on an overstocked range, and their natural dispersion from an understocked one, is the only precision instrument known to deer management. (Quoted in Flader 1978, p. 176)

That is, the only precision instrument in land management is not an instrument at all but a part of the original, natural biota. Leopold's scientific biographer, Susan Flader, summarizes the evolution of Leopold's land management philosophy thus:

> Early in his career he had visualized the management arts and sciences developing to such an extent that it would be possible eventually to shape and maintain a controlled environment, but his experiences with deer convinced him that the land organism was too complex and dynamic ever to be fully comprehended or controlled and that management, however essential, was itself subject to the same hazardous consequences as the short-sighted actions it was intended to correct. His career thus seems an extended ironic dilemma. He was a man engaged in attempting to make adjustments in order to restore a self-adjusting system so that adjustments would be unnecessary. As he once expressed it, "In the long run we shall learn that there is no such thing as forestry, no such thing as game management. The only reality is an intelligent respect for, and adjustment to, the inherent tendency of land to produce life." (Flader 1978, p. 270— the internal quotation is from a 1934 book review Leopold published in the *Journal of Forestry*.)

Leopold's experience with Southwestern watersheds convinced him that in more-fragile areas all the parts of the original, naturally evolved ecosystem must be preserved in functional form if the long-term fecundity of the land is to be preserved. His experience managing game herds through the 1930s and 1940s convinced him that it was not possible, even in more resilient ecosystems, to compensate precisely for the elimination of all members of an important category of species like the large carnivores.

Leopold believed that the sand counties of Central Wisconsin are, like the arid Southwest, a particularly fragile ecosystem in which it is important to model land management practices more closely on the original, naturally evolved biota. What he and his family have done with their Sauk County farm is an extreme example of this, insofar as they took (or rather left) the land entirely out of production of traditional agricultural products to harvest only game (and, recently, some timber).

When the Leopold family bought the property in 1935, the shack stood next to a windbreak and a low hill with a few scattered maples and cedars. In front of the shack was an abandoned corn field. In pre-Columbian times, oak savannah was the dominant ecosystem in southern Wisconsin, northern mesic forest dominated in the central latitudes, and boreal forest was restricted to the far north. The shack is in a south-central location, making it appropriate, in terms of the naturalness of the result, to restore the land either to savannah or to mesic forest. The family did both. Along the entrance road and on the hill behind the shack, the Leopolds planted 16,000 white and red pines. Initial plantings were largely unsuccessful, so they planted overly dense stands in subsequent years. The result today is a dense stand that is being thinned. In the abandoned corn field, the Leopolds did one of the first prairie restorations. Working entirely by hand, and one six-foot square at a time, they removed existing vegetation and planted an assortment of indigenous grasses and wildflowers typical of the tall grass prairie of southern Wisconsin in pre-Columbian times.

The Leopolds' work nicely illustrates my earlier point about ecosystems that are more natural in result being less natural in genesis. The woods behind the shack look quite natural insofar as they are characteristic of the northern mesic forest and the trees are not planted in any discernible pattern (the Leopolds sometimes tossed handfuls of stone into the air, planting a tree wherever one fell). But the forest is entirely unnatural in genesis. Again, the prairie in front of the shack is much more natural in result than the abandoned corn field, yet the prairie is entirely unnatural in genesis (in fact, Nina Leopold Bradley, Leopold's daughter, says that it took years for a cross-hatch pattern, created by working in six-foot squares, to disappear).

The Leopold shack property continues to be managed for more natural results but often with use of highly artificial techniques. The original property is now managed as the Leopold Reserve by the Sand County Foundation, a private, nonprofit corporation. Biologist Nina Leopold Bradley and her husband, Charles Bradley (another biologist), moved to the property in 1976 to codirect research on the reserve. The original property is coupled with about 200 acres that Leopold's children have acquired and almost 1500 acres of adjacent properties where the Sand County Foundation has cooperative management agreements with the landowners. The reserve acreage is divided into three management categories: some areas are not actively managed at all (except insofar as deer are removed seasonally), in others, fire is the only management tool used, and, in still others, a menagerie of techniques is used. On the latter acreages, for example, clearings are sometimes made using mechanized equipment. Here again, a more natural result is achieved, but by using very artificial techniques. Similarly, one of Nina Bradley's projects involves restoring swaths of prairie grasses along county roads in the vicinity by using the following very artificial technique. A tractor is used to apply a pesticide that breaks down to inert organic compounds within twenty-four to forty-eight hours. Prairie grass seeds are then applied using the tractor and, with all of the exotic grasses poisoned out, they thrive. In this case, the result looks unnatural in origin insofar as the strips of prairie grass are precisely the width of the pesticide sprayer and seed dispersion implements, but the prairie grasses are more natural in result than the exotics they replace.[2]

On the shack property, the Leopolds have taken Aldo's notion of "biotic farming" to an extreme, but Leopold believed that every farmer, even those farming in rather resilient ecosystems, can and should engage in some "biotic farming." In the section of "The Land Ethic" on "Land Health and the A-B Cleavage" (1949, pp. 221–22), Leopold introduces the term "biotic farming" on the heels of a discussion of the "cleavage" in foresty and in wildlife management. In each land management area, Leopold writes, an "A group . . . regards the land as soil, and its function as commodity-production," whereas a "B group . . . regards the land as a biota, and its function as something broader." All Leopold's sympathies appear to be with the B group. With respect to forestry, he writes, "group A is quite content to grow trees like cabbages," whereas "Group B feels the stirrings of an ecological conscience" (p. 221). And, of "all these cleavages," he says, "we see repeated the same basic paradoxes: man the conqueror *versus* man the biotic citizen; science the sharpener of his sword *versus* science the searchlight on his universe; land the slave and servant *versus* land the collective organism" (p. 223). Characterizing the A side as "the conqueror" with a view of land as "the slave and servant" is clearly pejorative in the context of other passages from the essay.

Yet a paradox of a philosophical sort consists of a pair of apparently contradictory statements, each of which we have good reason to believe. This is what

---

2. Information in the preceding paragraphs is based on two visits I made to the Leopold Reserve, in 1988 and in 1993. I deeply appreciated Nina Leopold Bradley's talking with me and my students and turning me loose on the property to take slides for use in my classes.

made it appropriate for Leopold to italicize "versus" in the above passage. The preservation–conservation divide is a "paradox" to the extent that partisans of each mistakenly emphasize it to the exclusion of the other.

The forestry Leopold favors is definitely multiple use, not just sustained yield, because on Leopold's view sustained yield requires multiple use, especially in more fragile ecosystems; foresters must worry about the "whole series of secondary forest functions: wildlife, recreation, watersheds, wilderness areas" (1949, p. 221). One of the functions Leopold ascribes to wilderness is "wilderness for recreation," but, given that he lists recreation separately in the sentence just quoted, "wilderness for wildlfe" (pp. 198–99)—that is, the preservation of biotic diversity—probably was foremost in his mind when he wrote this passage. That is, the lessons Leopold learned managing Southwestern watersheds pointed in the direction of policies that create no sharp dichotomy between national forests (the paradigm place for conservation) on the one hand and wilderness and national parks (the paradigm places for preservation) on the other.

Although he says less about farming than forestry, Leopold treats them analogously. His land management philosophy implies that, in more-fragile ecosystems, farming and ranching practices should more closely approximate the original, naturally evolved biota. But, even in the most resilient systems, farmers can and should play a role in the preservation of natural biota, as his remarks about biotic farming indicate. Leopold coined the term "biotic farming" in a 1939 *Journal of Forestry* article, "A Biotic View of Land." There, in a passage that became part of "The Land Ethic" (1949, p. 222), he wrote: "Agriculture, the most important land use, shows the least evidence of discontent with pioneering concepts. Conservation, among agricultural thinkers, still means conservation of the soil, rather than of the biota including the soil." This dramatically conveys Leopold's view that conservation and preservation interpenetrate on the farm. In urging conservation not just of soil but of "the biota," Leopold emphasizes that every farmer can contribute to the preservation of components of the original, naturally evolved ecosystem and that conservation is inadequate without this admixture of preservation:

> Biotic farming (if I may coin such a term) . . . would employ all native wild species not actually incompatible with tame ones. These species would include not merely game but rather the largest possible diversity of flora and fauna.
> Biotic farming, in short, would include wild plants and animals with tame ones as expressions of fertility.

And Leopold urges us to reconceive "the good farm" as in part an exercise in preservation:

> To accomplish such a revolution in the landscape, there must of course be a corresponding revolution in the landholder. The farmer who now seeks merely

> to preserve the soil must take account of the superstructure as well; a good farm must be one where the wild fauna and flora has lost acreage without losing its existence. (1991a, p. 272)

In short, it is good to adapt agricultural practices to the original, naturally evolved biota. At an extreme, this means "farming" the local biota themselves, as the Leopolds have done on their Sauk County farm. But, at a minimum, it means farming in ways that do not drive the original flora and fauna entirely off the land.

Leopold's emphasis on "biotic farming" in effect adds multiple use to the farm's traditional emphasis on sustained yield. Just as Leopold draws no sharp distinction between national forests and wilderness (and national parks), he draws no sharp distinction between farming and forestry. And, although Leopold does not explicitly consider it, his views can be extended to suburban and urban landscaping practices. Had he lived, Leopold probably would have been among the first to endorse the use of indigenous plants in landscaping.

To sum up, the conservation–preservation distinction usually is represented as parallel to two dichotomies: anthropocentrism versus biocentrism and "natural" versus "unnatural" management practices. However, growing scientific understanding of ecosystem functioning can lead to convergence between these perspectives. As we learn more about the role of special habitats such as wetlands in various ecological processes, it becomes increasingly reasonable, from an axiologically anthropocentric perspective, to leave such special habitats undeveloped, especially when we have already filled most of them. Similarly, to the extent that Leopold was right that, in order to maintain the fecundity of more-fragile ecosystems such as those in the arid Southwest and the sand counties of Wisconsin, all the parts of the original, naturally evolved ecosystem must be preserved, the strategies of a conservationist will converge with those of a preservationist with respect to those lands. Both will embrace a sliding scale: the less resilient the ecosystem, the more important it is to approximate land management practices closely to the original biota; the more resilient the system, the more we can be satisfied with just preserving remnant populations. Leopold believed that Southwestern watersheds and the sand counties of Wisconsin are examples of the former and that Europe and Japan are examples of the latter.

SAFEGUARDING THE PURSUIT OF GROUND PROJECTS

The biocentric individualist stance articulated in chapters 2–4 is axiologically anthropocentric, because it includes the principle that the satisfaction of ground projects that only (or very nearly only) humans have creates more value than the satisfaction of any other kind of interest. With reference to the generic argument with which I began this chapter, the specific version this stance implies is the following:

(1) Safeguarding the context in which future generations of humans can successfully prosecute their ground projects is a good (indeed, a very good!) thing.

(2) Safeguarding the successful prosecution of the ground projects of future generations requires us to pursue the goals listed on the environmentalist agenda.

(3) Therefore, pursuing the goals listed on the environmentalist agenda is a good (indeed, a very good!) thing.

Because the principles defended in chapter 4 do not imply statements about duties, this version of our generic argument does not conclude with an impressive-sounding statement that we ought to pursue the goals listed on the environmentalist agenda. The conclusion is only that this would be a very good thing. But, to paraphrase Aristotle, applied ethicists should seek perfect duties only to the extent that the nature of the case allows (Nicomachean Ethics, 1094b25). To show that safeguarding the pursuit of their ground projects by future generations is a very good thing is to show that dooming those projects would be a very bad thing. And what more could an environmentalist want or need than the conclusion that not pursuing the goals on the environmentalist agenda would be a very bad thing? In light of the difficulties for operationalizing utilitarianism discussed in chapter 4, I do not see any way to conclude that settling any particular real-world dispute a certain way would be wrong, nor even that pursuit of the general goals on the environmentalist agenda would be right. So I do not see what more one can ask than to show that pursuing these goals is a very good thing.

I also cannot claim that the foregoing discussion of preservation and conservation in various contexts—from the wilderness to the farm (and the city)—settles many particular real-world disputes about land use. The recognition that ecosystems lie on a continuum of appropriate management strategies does not settle questions about which areas lie where on the continuum. In forestry, for example, it might be preferable to manage some more resilient ecosystems very intensively, even in monocrop rotations, if this relieves pressure on other, more-fragile areas (e.g., remaining old growth in the Pacific Northwest). Similarly, intensive, monocrop agriculture may be the highest and best use for much of the Great Plains of North America if it frees other, more-fragile areas (such as the arid Southwest) from heavier exploitation. On the other hand, some foresters and agronomists believe that monocrop methods are inherently unsustainable in the long term, whatever the region. If they are right, then it would be better ultimately to abandon monocrop agriculture althogether. I do not know enough to decide questions of this sort. These are the kinds of issues that are, as I say at the beginning of this chapter, more raised than answered by the fact that all sides embrace the generic argument with which I began. But the foregoing discussion does illustrate how an individualist and axiologically anthropocentric view like mine can embrace the goals on the environmentalist agenda.

The preceding discussion of preservation and conservation is directly relevant to the first two goals on the environmentalist agenda:

1. preservation of species, wilderness, and special habitats such as wetlands, estuaries, rain forests and deserts; and
2. reintroduction of locally extinct species, including large predators, removal of exotic species, and adaptation of agricultural and landscaping practices to the local biota.

If lessons 4 and 5 of Leopold's mature land management philosophy are correct, then safeguarding humans' continued prosecution of their ground projects requires preservation everywhere of remnants of the original naturally evolved biota and, in more-fragile ecosystems, approximation of land-use practices to them. If this is true, then any axiological anthropocentrist can agree that we need to pursue these first two goals on the environmentalist agenda. As just noted, there will remain disagreement about how specifically to pursue these goals, but I do not think it is the philosopher's role to be the final arbiter of such specific policy questions.

I conclude this chapter by discussing briefly the remaining two goals. There is, first, goal 3: "substantial reduction of the global human population." How many human beings, successfully prosecuting ground projects, can the earth support? This is largely an empirical question, and I do not want to pretend that as a philosopher I am, by training, particularly competent to answer it. However, if it is true that safeguarding the continued prosecution of their ground projects by humans requires preservation everywhere of remnants of the original, naturally evolved biota and, in more-fragile ecosystems, approximation of land-use practices to them, then it is certainly very difficult to see how continued growth in the global human population is consistent with the pursuit of these goals. While I think that skeptics like Julian Simon are correct to point out that the limits to growth are not chiseled in tablets the way much of the catastrophist rhetoric of the 1970s environmental movement implied, it is utopian to suggest that we can successfully pursue the first and second goals on the environmentalist agenda while allowing continued growth of the global human population. Our numbers are still growing exponentially, and even if our population were capped at some present or near-future level, it is difficult to see how we could effectively share the planet with its premodern biota. In a 1986 article, Peter Vitousek, Paul and Anne Ehrlich, and Pamela Matson use various estimates of global human consumption of the earth's primary productivity (total energy captured through photosynthesis, after subtracting respiration by plant life on the planet) to estimate what percentage human beings appropriate. They conclude that

> about 40% of the present net primary production in terrestrial ecosystems is being co-opted by human beings each year. People use this material directly or indirectly [via domesticated animals], it flows to different consumers and decomposers than it otherwise would, or it is lost because of human-caused changes in land use. (Vitousek et al. 1986, p. 372)

If this estimate is even roughly in the ballpark, then accepting the first and second goals on the environmentalist agenda provides a prima facie case for accepting the third goal.

The final goal on the environmentalist agenda is "reduced reliance on chemicals in agriculture and reduced air and water emissions." Here again, to decide "How clean is clean enough?" would require answers to many empirical questions. But, certainly, when viewed from the beginning of the contemporary environmental movement (roughly the 1960s), substantial reductions are called for on anthropocentric grounds. Since then, integrated pest management has become endorsed in almost all quarters. This has led to substantially reduced reliance on chemicals in agriculture. The Clean Air and Clean Water Acts and amendments have substantially reduced air and water emissions. No doubt many in the environmental movement were thinking biocentrically when they endorsed them, but the success and breadth of these reforms suggests that many others endorsed them on anthopocentric grounds. What further reductions in chemical use and air and water emissions are called for, I cannot say. But if it is true that safeguarding the pursuit of the most important interests of human beings requires further reductions, then an axiologically anthropocentric view such as mine supports the conclusion that those reductions are a good, indeed a very good thing.

Two Dogmas of Environmental Ethics

MY GOAL in this book is twofold. First, in chapters 2–4, I articulate a biocentric individualist stance in ways that improve over previous articulations. Second, in chapters 5 and 6, I expose two dogmas of environmental ethics: that animal rights philosophies and axiologically anthropocentric views are antithetical to the environmentalist agenda.

In a widely reprinted article, J. Baird Callicott recommends that "environmental ethics" be "defined ostensively" using Leopold's thought:

> Partly because it is so new to Western philosophy (or at least heretofore only scarcely represented) *environmental ethics* has no precisely fixed conventional definition in glossaries of philosophical terminology. Aldo Leopold, however, is universally recognized as the father or founding genius of recent environmental ethics. His "land ethic" has become a modern classic and may be treated as the standard example, the paradigm case, as it were, of what an environmental ethic is. *Environmental ethics* then can be defined ostensively by using Leopold's land ethic as the exemplary type. I do not mean to suggest that all environmental ethics should necessarily conform to Leopold's paradigm, but the extent to which an ethical system resembles Leopold's land ethic might be used, for want of anything better, as a criterion to measure the extent to which it is nor is not of the environmental sort. (1980, p. 311)

As I detail above in the introduction and in chapters 1 and 5, Callicott was then, and remains, convinced that environmental holism is the distinguishing characteristic of Leopold's thought, the characteristic that makes his thought uniquely suited to justify pursuit of the goals on the environmentalist agenda. But, if Norton's reading of him is correct, Leopold himself recognized that an axiological anthropocentrist can embrace the environmentalist agenda.

My justification of the environmentalist agenda from an axiologically anthropocentric stance hinges on the truth of an empirical claim: safeguarding future human generations' pursuit of their most important interests requires us to pursue the goals on that agenda. This claim could turn out to be false. It is, however, widely accepted. Both environmentalists in general and Aldo Leopold in particular assume that it is true. But, if this empirical claim is true, then environmental holists cannot claim a monopoly on the "environmentally correct" ethics. As I show in chapters 5 and 6, individualist and axiologically anthropocentric views, such as the version of biocentric individualism elaborated and defended in this book, can also support the environmentalist agenda.

To identify environmental ethics with specifically holistic theories, as most thinkers in the field continue to do, is to deny that thinkers such as John Passmore, Bryan Norton, Richard Watson, and Paul Taylor (not to mention myself!) are doing environmental ethics. This strikes me as every bit as arbitrary as denying that environmental ethicists are really "doing philosophy." Environmental ethicists should have learned not to define the opposition out of the discipline. For too long, "pure" philosophers succeeded in doing this with "applied" ethicists in general and with environmental ethicists in particular.

The philosophical spade work I undertake in this book does not answer many practical, real-world policy issues. The recognition that axiological anthropocentrists and animal rightists can support the environmentalist agenda does not tell us what specific land management, population, or pollution policies to adopt. As I say in chapter 6, it raises these questions more than it answers them; it directs our attention to the core statements in Leopold's mature land management philosophy and focuses attention on their implementation. But, as I say at the end of the introduction, as a philosopher concerned about our treatment of both animals and the environment, I feel that I have done enough if I have shown that a serious commitment to improving both can spring from the same source.

References

Allen, Colin, and Mark Bekoff. 1994. "Function, Natural Design, and Animal Behavior: Philosophical and Ethological Considerations." In N. Thompson, ed., *Perspectives in Ethology, Vol. 11: Behavioral Design*, pp. 1–47. New York: Plenum Press.

Alloway, Thomas M. 1972. "Learning and Memory in Insects." *Annual Review of Entomology* 17:43–56.

Anscombe, G. E. M. 1963. *Intention*, 2d edition. Ithaca: Cornell University Press.

Arbor, J. L. 1986. "Animal Chauvinism, Plant-Regarding Ethics, and the Torture of Trees." *Australasian Journal of Philosophy* 64:335–39.

Attfield, Robin. 1981. "The Good of Trees." *Journal of Value Inquiry* 15:39–40.

———. *The Ethics of Environmental Concern*. New York: Columbia University Press.

Babbitt, Bruce. 1987. "The Land Ethic: A Guide for the World." In Thomas Tanner, ed., *Aldo Leopold: The Man and His Legacy*, pp. 137–42. Ankeny, Iowa: Soil Conservation Society of America.

Bak, Per, and Kan Chen. 1991. "Self-Organized Criticality." *Scientific American* 264:46–53.

Barrett, Stephen W. 1981. "The Relationship of Indian-Caused Fires to the Ecology of Western Montana Forests." M. S. thesis, 1981, University of Montana.

Bateson, Patrick. 1991. "Assessment of Pain in Animals." *Animal Behavior* 42:827–39.

Bean, Marian. 1991. "Environmental Groups and Animal Rights." *Alliance News* 8, no. 1 (February):6.

Bechtel, William, and Adele Abrahamsen. 1991. *Connectionism and the Mind: An Introduction to Parallel Processing in Networks*. Cambridge, Mass.: Basil Blackwell.

Bitterman, M. E. 1965. "The Evolution of Intelligence." *Scientific American* 212: 92–100.

———. 1988. "Vertebrate-Invertebrate Comparisons." In H. J. Jerison and I. Jerison, eds., *Intelligence and Evolutionary Biology*, pp. 251–76. Berlin: Springer-Verlag.

Boorse, Christopher. 1984. "Wright on Functions." In Elliott Sober, ed., *Conceptual Issues in Evolutionary Biology*, pp. 369–85. Cambridge, Mass.: MIT Press.

Brandt, Richard. 1979. *A Theory of the Good and the Right*. Oxford: Clarendon Press.

Bratman, Michael E. *Intention, Plans, and Practical Reason*. Cambridge: Harvard University Press, 1987.

Browne, Malcolm W. 1991. "New Animal Vaccines Spread Like Diseases." *New York Times*, 11 November 1991, pp. B5, B7.

Callicott, J. Baird 1980. "Animal Liberation: A Triangular Affair." *Environmental Ethics* 2: 311–38.

―――. 1986. "The Search for an Environmental Ethic." In Tom Regan, ed., *Matters of Life and Death*, 2d edition, pp. 381–423. New York: Random House.

―――. 1987. "The Conceptual Foundations of the Land Ethic." In J. Baird Callicott, ed., *Companion to "A Sand County Almanac"*, pp. 186–217. Madison: University of Wisconsin Press.

―――. 1989. "Animal Liberation and Environmental Ethics: Back Together Again." In *In Defense of the Land Ethic*, pp. 49–59. Albany: State University of New York Press.

―――. 1990. "Standards of Conservation: Then and Now." *Conservation Biology* 4:229–32.

―――. 1992. "Aldo Leopold's Metaphor." In Robert Costanza, Bryan Norton, and Benjamin Haskell, eds., *Ecosystem Health: New Goals for Environmental Management*, pp. 42–56. Washington, D.C.: Island Press.

―――. 1994. "Moral Monism in Environmental Ethics Defended." *Journal of Philosophical Research* 19:51–60.

Chase, Alston. 1986. *Playing God in Yellowstone.* San Diego: Harcourt Brace Jovanovich.

Comstock, Gary, ed. 1994. "Might Morality Require Veganism?" Special issue of *Journal of Agricultural and Environmental Ethics.*

Conniff, Richard. 1990. "Fuzzy Wuzzy Thinking about Animal Rights." *Audubon* 92, no. 6 (November 1990):120–33.

Creed, William, et al. 1984. "Harvest Management: The Wisconsin Experience." In Lowell K. Halls, ed., *White-Tailed Deer Ecology and Management*, pp. 211–42. Harrisburg, Pa.: Stackpole Books.

Cronon, William. 1983. *Changes in the Land.* New York: Hill and Wang.

Darwin, Charles. 1874. *The Descent of Man.* 2d edition. New York: Hurst and Co.

DeGrazia, David, and Andrew Rowan. 1991. "Pain, Suffering, and Anxiety in Animals and Humans." *Theoretical Medicine* 12:193–211.

Donald, Merlin. 1991. *Origins of the Modern Human Mind: Three Stages in the Evolution of Culture and Cognition.* Cambridge, Mass.: Harvard University Press.

Dretske, Fred. 1995. *Naturalizing the Mind.* Cambridge, Mass.: MIT Press.

Eisemann, C. H., et al. 1984. "Do Insects Feel Pain?: A Biological View." *Experientia* 40: 164–67.

Feinberg, Joel. 1974. "The Rights of Animals and Unborn Generations." In William T. Blackstone, ed., *Philosophy and Environmental Crisis*, pp. 43–68. Athens: University of Georgia Press.

―――. 1984. *Harm to Others: The Moral Limits of the Criminal Law.* New York: Oxford University Press.

Fiorito, Graziano, and Pietro Scotto. 1992. "Observational Learning in *Octopus vulgaris.*" *Science* 256:545–47.

Finsen, Susan. 1990. "On Moderation." In Marc Bekoff and Dale Jamieson, eds., *Interpretation and Explanation in the Study of Animal Behavior*, pp. 394–419. Boulder: Westview Press.

Flader, Susan. 1978. *Thinking Like a Mountain: Aldo Leopold and the Evolution of an Ecological Attitude toward Deer, Wolves, and Forests.* Lincoln: University of Nebraska Press.

Frey, R. G. 1980. *Interests and Rights: The Case against Animals.* Oxford: Clarendon Press.

Fodor, Jerry, and Zenon Pylyshyn. 1988. "Connectionism and Cognitive Architecture: A Critical Analysis." *Cognition* 28:3–71.

Fuster, Joaquin M. 1989. *The Prefrontal Cortex: Anatomy, Physiology, and Neuropsychology of the Frontal Lobe,* 2d edition. New York: Raven Press.

Goodpaster, Kenneth. 1978. "On Being Morally Considerable." *Journal of Philosophy* 75: 308–25.

———. 1980. "On Stopping at Everything: A Reply to W. M. Hunt." *Environmental Ethics* 2:281–84.

Griffin, Donald. 1992. *Animal Minds.* Chicago: University of Chicago Press.

Hare, R. M. 1981. *Moral Thinking: Its Levels, Method, and Point.* New York: Oxford University Press.

Hargrove, Eugene C. 1989. *Foundations of Environmental Ethics.* Englewood Cliffs, N.J.: Prentice-Hall.

Hargrove, Eugene C., ed. 1992. *The Animal Rights/Environmental Ethics Debate: The Environmental Perspective.* Albany: State University of New York Press.

Harlow, John M. 1868. "Recovery from the Passage of an Iron Bar through the Head." *Publications of the Massachusetts Medical Society* 2:327–47.

Hebb, D. O. 1946. "Emotion in Man and Animal: An Analysis of the Intuitive Processes of Recognition." *Psychological Review* 53:88–106.

Hume, David. 1957 [1751]. *An Inquiry concerning the Principles of Morals.* Edited by Charles W. Hendel. Indianapolis: Bobbs-Merrill.

———. 1978 [1739–40]. *A Treatise of Human Nature,* 2d edition. New York: Oxford University Press.

IUCN. 1980. *World Conservation Strategy: Living Resource Conservation for Sustainable Development.* Moges, Switzerland: International Union for Conservation of Nature and Natural Resources.

James, William. 1948. "The Moral Philosopher and the Moral Life." In *Essays in Pragmatism,* pp. 65–87. New York: Hafner.

Jamieson, Dale. 1990. "Rights, Justice, and Duties to Provide Assistance." *Ethics* 100:349–62.

Katz, Eric. 1990. "Defending the Use of Animals by Business: Animal Liberation and Environmental Ethics." In W. Michael Hoffman, Robert Frederick, and Edward S. Petry Jr., eds., *Business, Ethics, and the Environment: The Public Policy Debate,* pp. 223–32. New York: Quorum Books.

Leopold, Aldo. 1933. *Game Management.* New York: Charles Scribner.

———. 1949. *A Sand County Almanac.* New York: Oxford University Press.

———. 1979. "Some Fundamentals of Conservation in the Southwest." *Environmental Ethics* 1:131–41.

———. 1990. "Means and Ends in Wildlife Management." *Environmental Ethics* 12:329–32.

————. 1991a [1939]. "A Biotic View of Land." In Susan Flader and J. Baird Callicott, eds., *The River of the Mother of God and Other Essays by Aldo Leopold*, pp. 266–73. Madison: University of Wisconsin Press.

————. 1991b [1944]. "Conservation: In Whole or in Part?" In Susan Flader and J. Baird Callicott, eds., *The River of the Mother of God and Other Essays by Aldo Leopold*, pp. 310–19. Madison: University of Wisconsin Press.

————. 1991c [1941]. "Wilderness as a Land Laboratory." In Susan Flader and J. Baird Callicott, eds., *The River of the Mother of God and Other Essays by Aldo Leopold*, pp. 287–89. Madison: University of Wisconsin Press.

Leopold, A. Starker, et al. 1963. "Study of Wildlife Problems in National Parks." *Twenty-eighth North American Wildlife Conference* 28:28–45.

Levin, Luis E., and Enrique Vergara. 1987. "Reversal Learning in Groups of the Schooling Fish *Aphyocharax erithrurus* on an Avoidance Paddle." *Journal of Comparative Psychology* 1010:317–21.

Luria, Aleksandr. 1966. *Higher Cortical Functions in Man*. Translated by Basil Haigh. New York: Basic Books.

Martin, Michael. 1990. "Ecosabotage and Civil Disobedience." *Environmental Ethics* 12: 291–310.

McCullough, Dale. 1979. *The George Reserve Deer Herd: Population Ecology of a K-Selected Species*. Ann Arbor: University of Michigan Press.

————. 1984. "Lessons from the George Reserve." In Lowell K. Halls, ed., *White-Tailed Deer Ecology and Management*, pp. 211–42. Washington, D.C.: Wildlife Management Institute.

————. 1987. "North American Deer Ecology: Fifty Years Later." In Thomas Tanner, ed., *Aldo Leopold: The Man and His Legacy*, pp. 115–22. Ankeny, Iowa: Soil Conservation Society of America.

McKibben, Bill. 1989. *The End of Nature*. New York: Random House.

Meine, Curt. 1988. *Aldo Leopold: His Life and Work*. Madison: University of Wisconsin Press.

Midgley, Mary. 1983. "Duties concerning Islands." *Encounter* 60: 36–43.

Millikan, Ruth. 1984. *Language, Thought and Other Biological Categories*. Cambridge, Mass.: MIT Press, Bradford Books.

Naess, Arne. 1973. "The Shallow and the Deep, Long-Range Ecology Movement: A Summary." *Inquiry* 16:95–100.

Nagel, Ernest. 1961. *The Structure of Science: Problems in the Logic of Scientific Explanation*. London: Routledge and Kegan Paul.

Nagel, Thomas. 1974. "What Is It Like to Be a Bat?" *Philosophical Review* 83:435–50.

Nash, Roderick. 1989. *The Rights of Nature*. Madison: University of Wisconsin Press.

Neander, Karen. 1991. "The Teleological Notion of 'Function.'" *Australasian Journal of Philosophy* 69:444–68.

Nolte, John. 1981. *The Human Brain: An Introduction to Its Functional Anatomy*. St. Louis: C. V. Mosby.

Norton, Bryan. 1986. "Conservation and Preservation: A Conceptual Rehabilitation." *Environmental Ethics* 8:195–220.

————. 1987. *Why Preserve Natural Variety?* Princeton: Princeton University Press.

———. 1988. "The Constancy of Leopold's Land Ethic." *Conservation Biology* 2:93–102.

———. 1990. "Context and Hierarchy in Aldo Leopold's Theory of Environmental Management." *Ecological Economics* 2:199–227.

———. 1991. *Toward Unity among Environmentalists.* New York: Oxford University Press.

———. 1992. "A New Paradigm for Environmental Management." In Robert Costanza and Bryan Norton, eds., *Ecosystem Health: New Goals for Environmental Management*, pp. 23–41. Washington, D.C.: Island Press.

Odum, Eugene. 1983. *Basic Ecology.* Philadelphia: Sanders College Publishing.

Ortega y Gasset, José. 1985. *Meditations on Hunting.* New York: Charles Scribner's Sons.

Passmore, John. 1974. *Man's Responsibility for Nature.* New York: Charles Scribner's Sons.

Perry, Ralph Barton. 1926. *General Theory of Value.* New York: Longman's, Green, and Co.

Rawls, John. 1971. *A Theory of Justice.* Cambridge, Mass.: Harvard University Press.

Regan, Tom. 1976. "Feinberg on What Sorts of Beings Can Have Rights." *Southern Journal of Philosophy* 14:485–97.

———. 1981. "The Nature and Possibility of an Environmental Ethic." *Environmental Ethics* 3:19–34.

———. 1983. *The Case for Animal Rights.* Berkeley: University of California Press.

Richards, Graham 1987. *Human Evolution: An Introduction for the Behavioural Sciences.* London: Routledge and Kegan Paul.

Rollin, Bernard. 1981. *Animal Rights and Human Morality.* Buffalo: Prometheus Books.

———. 1989. *The Unheeded Cry.* New York: Oxford University Press.

Rolston, Holmes III. 1974–75. "Is There an Ecological Ethic?" *Ethics* 85:93–109.

———. 1988. *Environmental Ethics: Duties to and Values in the Natural World.* Philadelphia: Temple University Press.

Rose, Margaret, and David Adams. 1989. "Evidence for Pain and Suffering in Other Animals." In Gill Langley, ed., *Animal Experimentation: The Consensus Changes*, pp. 42–71. New York: Chapman and Hall.

Routley, Richard. 1973. "Is There a Need for a New, an Environmental Ethic?" In *Proceedings of the XVth World Congress of Philosophy.* Varna, Bulgaria.

Russow, Lilly-Marlene. 1981. "Why Do Species Matter?" *Environmental Ethics* 3:101–12.

Sagoff, Mark. 1984. "Animal Liberation and Environmental Ethics: Bad Marriage, Quick Divorce." *Osgood Hall Law Journal* 22:297–307.

Schweitzer, Albert. 1955. *The Philosophy of Civilization.* New York: Macmillan.

Shepard, Paul. 1973. *The Tender Carnivore and the Sacred Game: The Human Past as the Key to Modern Man's Identity—and to His Future.* New York: Charles Scribner's Sons.

Shue, Henry. 1980. *Basic Rights: Subsistence, Affluence, and U.S. Foreign Policy.* Princeton: Princeton University Press.

Sidgwick, Henry.1893. *The Methods of Ethics.* London: Macmillan and Co.

Sierra Club, Lone Star Chapter. 1993. *State Capitol Report* 10, no. 5 (May 1):2.

Singer, Peter. 1990. *Animal Liberation*, 2d edition. New York: Avon Books.

———. 1993. *Practical Ethics*, 2d edition. Cambridge: Cambridge University Press.

Smith, Adam. 1976 [1759]. *Theory of the Moral Sentiments.* New York: Oxford University Press.

Smith, Jane A., and Kenneth M. Boyd, eds. 1991. *Lives in the Balance: The Ethics of Using Animals in Biomedical Research*. New York: Oxford University Press.

Smith, Julie A. 1991. "Wisconsin Greens Support Hunting: The Alliance Wonders Why?" *Alliance News* 8, no. 1 (February):1, 7.

Sober, Elliott. 1980. "Evolution, Population Thinking, and Essentialism." *Philosophy of Science* 47: 350–83.

Spencer, Gary E. 1983. *Piney Woods Deer Management*. Texas Parks and Wildlife Department Bulletin 7000–88 (February 1983).

Stettner, Laurence Jay, and Kenneth A. Matyniak. 1980. "The Brain of Birds." In *Birds*, pp. 192–99. No editor. San Francisco: W. H. Freeman and Co.

Stone, Christopher D. 1972. "Should Trees Have Standing?" *Southern California Law Review* 45:450–502.

Tansley, Arthur G. 1920. "The Classification of Vegetation and the Concept of Development." *Journal of Ecology* 8:118–49.

———. 1935. "The Use and Abuse of Vegetational Concepts and Terms." *Ecology* 16: 284–307.

Taylor, Paul. 1986. *Respect for Nature: A Theory of Environmental Ethics*. Princeton: Princeton University Press.

Tecce, Joseph, and Neil Scheff. 1969. "Attention Reduction and Suppressed Direct-Current Potentials in the Human Brain." *Science* 164:331–33.

Thomson, Garrett. 1987. *Needs*. London: Routledge and Kegan Paul.

VanDeVeer, Donald. 1979. "Interspecific Justice." *Inquiry* 22:55–70.

Varner, Gary E. 1985. "The Schopenhauerian Challenge in Environmental Ethics." *Environmental Ethics* 7:209–29.

———. 1987. "Do Species Have Standing?" *Environmental Ethics* 9:57–72.

———. 1990. "Biological Functions and Biologial Interests." *Southern Journal of Philosophy* 28:251–70.

———. 1994. "The Prospects for Consensus and Convergence in the Animal Rights Debate." *Hastings Center Report* 24, no. 1 (January/February): 23–27.

Vitousek, Peter M., et al. 1986. "Human Appropriation of the Products of Photosynthesis." *Bioscience* 36:368–73.

Walter, W. Grey, et al. 1964. "Contingent Negative Variation: An Electric Sign of Sensorimotor Association and Expectancy in the Human Brain." *Nature* 203: 380–84.

Wells, M. J. 1978. *Octopus: Physiology and Behavior of an Advanced Invertebrate*. London: Chapman and Hall.

Wenz, Peter. 1988. *Environmental Justice*. Albany: State University of New York Press.

Williams, Bernard. 1973. *Problems of the Self*. Cambridge: Cambridge University Press.

———. 1981. *Moral Luck*. Cambridge: Cambridge University Press.

Wisconsin DNR. 1987. *Wisconsin Game and Fur Harvest Summary, 1930–1986*. Madison: Wisconsin Department of Natural Resources.

Wright, Larry. 1976. *Teleological Explanations*. Berkeley: University of California Press.

Yakovlev, P. I., and A. R. Lecours. 1967. "The Myelogenetic Cycles of Regional Maturation of the Brain." In Alexandre Minkowski, ed., *Regional Development of the Brain in Early Life*, pp. 3–70. Philadelphia: F. A. Davis.

Index

Proper names are included only where the individuals and/or their works are discussed in the text—if an author's name appears only in a parenthetical citation, it is not indexed; however, all cited works appear in the list of references.

DATE DUE
